Rediscovering
New Testament
Fellowship

REDISCOVERING NEW TESTAMENT FELLOWSHIP

Thomas J. Madon

DEDICATION

With this being a book about Christians coming together in small groups to experience the church through embracing the *one another's,* the most appropriate person to receive the dedication is my faithful wife, Linda. She has always enthusiastically and generously opened our home to the countless guests and small groups we have hosted over these many years. I can say beyond any shadow of a doubt that any guest who has entered our home has been a recipient of her love and grace. My life and ministry have been enriched through her in immeasurable ways that cannot be described with words. She has been and continues to be the consummate helper to me and to the ministry we have shared for nearly six decades. Even now she often plays the piano for our worship team at church, and her fluency in Spanish is an incredible blessing as we minister to our sister churches in Mexico. She is also loved dearly by the younger women she faithfully prays for and mentors. Linda is the loving mother to our adult children and dearest friends: Cheryl, Scott, and Christy, as well the devoted grandmother to Lauren, Nathan, Ashlyn, Trent, Brooke, Seth, Ainsley and Allyse. Our great-grandchildren, Ian, Brielle, and Asher have brought even greater joy in these last few years.

"An excellent wife, who can find? For her worth is far above jewels. The heart of her husband trusts in her, and he will have no lack of gain. She does him good and not evil all the days of her life" (Proverbs 31:10-12).

2

ACKNOWLEDGMENTS

Only those who have written a book can fully appreciate all that is involved, beginning with those who urge you to write. While several friends suggested a book on the *one another's*, my friend, Paul Sargent, has shown the most consistent interest. From the time he saw my initial studies on this topic in the late 1980s, and on several occasions since, he has enthusiastically affirmed the immense value of the one another's, using my lessons in various small groups. Thank you, Paul!

As with my first book, *Because of Grace,* our daughter, Cheryl Helliwell, provided suggestions and assisted with the cover design. She and her husband, James, also provided valuable assistance in the final steps leading up to submitting it for publication. Thank you, Cheryl and James, for taking time out of your busy lives to help your dad!

My proofreaders were Audrey Bush and Elizabeth Amos, loyal friends from LifePoint Church, a place we will always affectionately refer to as our church in Indiana. Both are teachers who excel in their profession. Thank you, ladies, for this labor of love to your aging pastor!

My daily helper, encourager, proofreader, and faithful grammar consultant has been my wife, Linda, who daily affirms the value of the content by embracing the one another's as a way of life.

TABLE OF CONTENTS

PREFACE

I was introduced to the One Another commands of the New Testament in the early 1970s while serving as Campus Director at San Jose State University with Campus Crusade for Christ. One of my coworkers and friends, Greg Gripentrog, had moved to Texas with his wife, Denyse, to enroll at Dallas Seminary in preparation for a life of ministry in missions. One of his first classes was taught by Dr. Gene Getz, who gave his students a list of the 58 one another's, along with references. Because Greg and I had partnered in ministry as brothers in Christ, he mailed a copy to me, believing I would respond to them, and he was correct. From the moment I saw the list, I was captivated. My initial thought was how the one another's provided Biblical reinforcement for what we were already witnessing in the lives of our college students. When a new Christian became involved in a small group with other believers, their spiritual growth accelerated as they experienced fellowship around the one another's with God's Word as the central focus.

In 1974, Dr. Getz published what would become a landmark book, entitled *Sharpening the Focus of the Church.* While the emphasis was broader in scope, the book provided greater understanding than the simple one another list I had received from Greg. By this time I had returned to pastoral ministry, serving on the staff of Grace Community Church in Tyler, Texas, where I had previously been a youth pastor. Grace Community had also been our primary supporting church during the four years we spent in campus ministry. The church invited us to return, stating that they observed pastoral gifts in me, and we gladly accepted, believing this was God's will for our future.

Our ministry with Campus Crusade had been fruitful, but also indispensable for our continued growth as a couple. Linda and I became more confident in sharing the gospel, in discipling others,

5

while also discovering how to open our home as a base for ministry. As a result of biblical teaching on the family by Dr. Howard Hendricks, God also brought a needed renewal to our marriage, and for that we are eternally grateful. One of my observations during those years was that the students who thrived spiritually were also involved in a local church, and my heart was being progressively drawn to serving again as a pastor, having ministered part-time as a student during my last year of college and four years of seminary.

Another influential book was forthcoming from Dr. Getz, *Building Up One Another,* the first of several exploring in greater detail the significance of the one another's to relational health in the church. He also planted Fellowship Bible Church in Dallas, and from there several other congregations were spawned. Because Dr. Getz's biblical insights had influenced me so deeply, in the mid-1990s I invited him to our church in Indianapolis to speak to the pastors in our network of community churches. His theme was the vital importance of the one another's to authentic fellowship.

As to my church involvement with the one another's, since completing our tenure with Campus Crusade in the summer of 1973, I have been blessed to serve as a pastor in three churches: 13 years at Grace Community Church in Tyler, Texas; 24 years at Community Church of Southport (now LifePoint Church) in Indianapolis, where I was the founding pastor, and, since 2010 at Living Word Fellowship in Porterville, CA, but only serving part-time in this autumn season of life. Our friends in those churches are aware of my passion for New Testament fellowship, and how I have sought to share the one another's through sermon series, Sunday school classes, Bible study guides for small groups, and various articles to our church family.

My motivation for writing this book is identical to 2019 when I composed my autobiography, *Because of Grace – The Personal and Pastoral Memoirs of One Called by Sovereign Grace from the Hills of Appalachia.* On that occasion, the persistent encouragement of friends and family prompted me to put in writing the narrative of how God's grace transformed my life, brought health to our marriage and family, and has been portrayed in our decades of ministry. In this instance, it was again the comments of those who responded positively to the material I taught on the one another's that encouraged me to put these truths into writing.

The first two chapters are foundational and introductory to the one another theme. In the first I seek to describe the rich essence of New Testament fellowship. The second explains the oft-overlooked significance of Jesus' New Commandment, introduced during His final Passover with His disciples. Both chapters are essential to understanding the ones that follow. The first two also highlight my thesis, namely, the one another's in the epistles have their origin in the example of Jesus, and in how He loved His initial disciples.

There are 58 one another commands in the New Testament, with *love one another,* the subject of chapter two, mentioned more frequently than any other. While each one is equally inspired and worthy of diligent study and application, in addition to *love one another,* I have written chapters on the 15 I view as most prominent.

While my prayer is that you will read the entire book, it may be helpful to know that chapters 3 through 16 may be read in any sequence, with each one standing on its own. These chapters were initially presented as sermons, though I have included additional material, along with making stylistic changes for this format.

With some of the one another's being so closely related, careful readers will recognize that I used some biblical passages more than once, simply because they have applications for more than one truth.

You will note that I have included discussion questions at the end of each chapter, and I encourage you to feel free to add others.

My hope is that some will be motivated to use the book in a small group with others in the church. If this is not possible, I suggest finding a reading partner with whom you may discuss the content, and especially how these biblical truths apply to your life.

As to my writing approach, my goal has been to carefully shine a light on what the New Testament says about each one another command. Because of this, the verses are written out, and not simply the references. While I make observations and share some of my experiences on each topic, my encouragement comes from knowing it is God's Word He has promised to honor and bless. "For as the rain and the snow come down from heaven, and do not return there without watering the earth and making it bear and sprout, and furnishing seed to the sower and bread to the eater; so will My word be which goes forth out of My mouth; it shall not return to Me empty, without accomplishing what I desire, and without succeeding in the matter for which I sent it" (Isaiah 55:10-11).

As you read, may God open your eyes to His truth, and may He give you a heart to apply these lifechanging principles in your relationships with others in God's forever family.

Because of grace,

Pastor Tom

Chapter One

New Testament Fellowship

"Two are better than one because they have a good return for their labor. For if either of them falls, the one will lift up his companion. But woe to the one who falls when there is not another to lift him up."

Ecclesiastes 4:9-10

Having served more than 50 years as a pastor, one of my continuing concerns has been the health of the church. Many pastors become enamored by growth, attending the latest seminars and enthusiastically devouring church growth books which promise foolproof methods to multiply the size of their congregations. My conviction, however, is that if a church is spiritually healthy, God will, in His time, bless that church with whatever growth He intends.

Because I believe in the authority and sufficiency of Scripture, discovering what makes for a healthy church begins with returning to the first-century church described in the book of Acts. As I have studied and reflected on that flourishing assembly of believers, several features have captured my attention. One is that the members of that church shared five vital experiences.[1]

- *Vital worship experiences* (singing, praying, giving, communion, preaching/teaching)

- *Vital learning experiences* (hearing and applying the Apostles' teaching)

9

- *Vital ministry experiences* (serving one another and others outside the church)

- *Vital witnessing experiences* (proclaiming the gospel to an unbelieving world)

- *Vital relational experiences* (experiencing New Testament fellowship)

The fifth, *vital relational experiences with one another,* the focus of this book, is captured in the word *fellowship - koinonia* in the Greek language. In describing this infant but already thriving church, Luke records, "They were continually devoting themselves to the apostles' teaching, and to fellowship, to the breaking of bread and to prayer" (Acts 2:42). It is not surprising that the apostles' teaching is mentioned as a high priority or that prayer and the Lord's Table be included in the list; all three are widely recognized requisites for spiritual health and growth. What is striking, however, is how the first-century church also *continually devoted themselves to fellowship.* As Jerry Bridges astutely points out, "They didn't just *have* fellowship; they *devoted* themselves to it."[2] Fellowship was just as high a priority as was their commitment to prayer, communion, and God's Word.

Fellowship, however, is one of those words whose original meaning has been substantially weakened from how it was understood and practiced in the New Testament church, a meaning that desperately needs to be *rediscovered.* For those of us who live in America, fellowship largely refers to a social gathering of Christians for *food, fun, and fellowship,* perhaps in the church *fellowship* hall. The tendency is to refer to any activity we have with other believers - playing games, talking about sports, politics, and other current events - as fellowship. While these activities can be enjoyable and at times beneficial, they fall far short of the spiritual bond and rich communion inherent in true *koinonia – New*

Testament fellowship. It is not only a tragic abuse of a robust New Testament word when we equate social activities with fellowship; it can also contribute to self-deception. While thinking we are experiencing fellowship, our inner persons may be starving for this significantly deeper way of relating which God Himself placed within each one of His children.

J. I. Packer writes, "Fellowship is one of the great words of the New Testament. It denotes something vital to the Christian's spiritual health, and central to the church's true life. It is of the first importance; therefore, we should be clear in our minds as to what Christian fellowship truly is."[3]

Different English words are used in the New Testament to translate *koinonia*: participation, partnership, sharing, and fellowship. Jerry Bridges explains that these various renderings of *koinonia* convey two related meanings: (1) to share in the joint sense of participation and (2) to share with, in the sense of giving what we have to others.[4]

To share in such a rich and meaningful way is possible because God first called us into a relationship (fellowship) with His Son. The Apostle Paul affirmed this at the beginning of his first letter to the church in Corinth: "God is faithful, through whom you were called into fellowship with His Son, Jesus Christ our Lord" (I Corinthians 1:9). The Apostle John passionately articulated this same truth: "What we have seen and heard we declare to you, so that you and we together may share in a common life, that life we share with God the Father and God the Son" (I John 1:3 *New English Bible*).[5] At its very essence, fellowship (*koinonia*) is sharing the common life of the Father and the Son, with other believers, through the indwelling Holy Spirit. True fellowship happens when I share with you out of the life I have graciously received from the Lord through His Word and by His Spirit, while at the same time receiving a measure of what you have also been given as a result of your relationship with Him.

11

The danger is to view fellowship as merely horizontal while overlooking that it is first vertical. It is as the Apostle John wrote, "Our fellowship is with the Father and with His Son, Jesus Christ" (I John 1:3). It is this personal fellowship with God that distinguishes us as Christians. The person without this vertical connection may experience and enjoy social interaction with Christians, but if he does not know Christ, true New Testament *koinonia* can never be experienced. Only when a person responds in faith to God's gracious call to salvation and into a personal relationship with Him does he have the capacity for rich and rewarding fellowship with other believers.

This relationship between Christians is characterized by constant giving and receiving from one another and is meant to be the norm for God's people. This means that New Testament fellowship, at its core, is not an activity, but a relationship, first with the Father, Son, and Holy Spirit, and then with other believers. When seen in this way, it is not a luxury. As J.I. Packer explains: "Such fellowship is a spiritual necessity; for God has made us in such a way that our fellowship with Him is fed by our fellowship with other Christians."[6]

Fellowship of this sort is what we see in the New Testament. It is the reciprocal, mutual family activity of God's children, one that involves giving as well as receiving. One refreshing example is in the Apostle Paul's letter to the church in Rome. Even though he had not yet traveled to that renowned city, Paul's words of anticipation capture this reciprocal feature of all New Testament fellowship. "For I long to see you so that I may impart some spiritual gift to you, that you may be established; that is, *that I may be encouraged together with you while among you, each of us by the other's faith, both yours and mine"* (Romans 1:11-12; italics mine). Being encouraged, each of us by the other's faith, is the essence of New Testament fellowship.

In describing this reciprocal truth, J. I. Packer provides this instructive insight: "Christian fellowship is an expression of both love and humility. It springs from a desire to bring benefit to others, coupled with a sense of personal weakness and need. It has a double motive – the wish to help and be helped; to edify and to be edified. It also has a double aim – to do, and to receive good. It is a corporate seeking by Christian people to know God better through sharing with each other what, individually, they have learned from Him already."[7]

After planting the church in Philippi on his second missionary journey, Paul used the word *koinonia* in describing his relational connection with the church: "I thank my God in all my remembrance of you, always offering prayer with joy in my every prayer for you all, in view of your *participation (koinonia)* in the gospel from the first day until now" (Philippians 1:3-5; italics mine). The church owed their very existence to Paul, recognizing him as their spiritual father; he was the one who brought them the gospel on his second missionary journey. Immediately afterward, because of their excitement over the life-changing power of the gospel, the church began to partner with Paul by giving to his ministry, including financially. In his letter to them, Paul expressed his sincere gratitude: "You yourselves also know, Philippians, that at the first preaching of the gospel, after I left Macedonia, no church shared with me in the matter of giving and receiving but you alone; for even in Thessalonica you sent a gift more than once for my needs" (Philippians 4:15-16).

The giving of material resources, such as the church in Philippi did with Paul, is one of the classic marks of *koinonia* in the New Testament – sharing one's material resources with others.[8] This was evident in the very beginning of the church as "all those who had believed were together and had all things in common; and they began selling their property and possessions and were sharing them with all, as anyone might have need" (Acts 2:44-45).

Paul later writes about "contributing to the needs of the saints" (Romans 12:13), and of how the church would be "enriched in everything for all liberality" and how "the ministry of this service is not only fully supplying the needs of the saints, but is also overflowing through many thanksgivings to God" (II Corinthians 9:11-12).

As I look back over the six-plus decades since responding to God's call on my life at the age of 16, on more occasions than I can recall, God graciously met my needs and those of my family through the generosity of His people. My wife and I, to this very day, treasure the devoted friends who loved and prayed for us but also invested their resources, *partnering* with us to such an extent that we could not have continued in our ministry without them. For their generous investment and faithful friendship, we are eternally grateful.

As the years have passed, we in turn have been able to contribute to others, *partnering* with them in their respective ministry callings, and what a rich blessing this has been. Those who generously give and invest their resources in other needy believers know from experience the truth of Jesus' words when He said, "It is more blessed to give than to receive" (Acts 20:35). New Testament fellowship assumes this willingness to serve others, generously investing in them out of the resources God has entrusted to us. Relationships having this type of depth are the expected outcome of sharing the common life of Christ who gave Himself for us.

Since first beginning to comprehend and be captured by New Testament fellowship in the early 1970s, I have sought to teach these truths in the three churches where I have served. While some have enthusiastically embraced the teaching and sought to pursue it, others have been reluctant. The result is that they have failed to experience the level of fellowship we see in the New Testament. While most enjoy interacting about the various "one another" admonitions which are the heart of this book, phrases that capture the essence of fellowship (koinonia), the experiencing of it is much more challenging. As I have prayerfully reflected as to why many

Christians are content to settle for a more superficial way of relating, I see certain factors that work against true fellowship.

One is our affluence. When compared to much of the world, Christians in America have far more comforts and conveniences, enabling us to get along well without feeling the need for this deeper level of relating. It is not that we do not love and appreciate our brothers and sisters in Christ, for it is obvious that we do. The reality is that our circumstances are such that we do not sense the need for fellowship (*koinonia*) to the same degree as believers in other parts of the world.

A second factor, often a byproduct of our affluence, is the individualistic, self-sufficient way many have in approaching life. To openly ask for help is viewed as a sign of weakness. Many of us believe we can solve our problems and survive on our own. This independent attitude works against the rich, relational connections experienced by the first-century church.

A third reason some resist this relational component of our faith is because of deep wounds from their past. In some instances, these occurred in their family of origin but in other cases from broken relationships in the body of Christ. Because of these emotional wounds, they are reluctant to interact with other believers, especially in more intimate settings where they may be asked to participate.

One encouraging glimpse of a deeper level of fellowship for me occurred in 2010 when my wife, Linda, and I had the opportunity to make two ministry trips to Cuba. As I was nearing retirement as pastor at LifePoint Church in Indianapolis after 24 years, a man in our church with a ministry in Cuba asked if we would join him and his wife in a ministry to pastors and their wives. My assignment would be to teach at a spring marriage retreat to several ministry couples in three different cities of that beautiful Caribbean island, the cities of Havana, Holguin, and Baracoa. Our friends also asked if we would return in the fall to the same three groups where my assignment would be to speak on pastoral leadership. God richly blessed those trips, and Linda and I will always cherish them among our ministry highlights.

One of our lasting impressions from these Cuban couples was how they loved meeting together but for more than social activities. Most had to walk or hitchhike long distances from their homes to reach the churches where we met. The homes from which they came were, out of necessity, often shared not only with their children but other family members: parents, grandparents, aunts, uncles, etc. Food for them is not nearly as plentiful and varied as it is for us, nor do they have the entertainment options such as we enjoy. As a result, the most anticipated events of their week were when they gathered with their brothers and sisters in Christ. During these times of singing, worship, prayer, listening, and responding to God's Word, along with sharing their lives over the staples of beans and rice, I sensed that they were coming closer to experiencing *New Testament fellowship* than many of us do in America.

After being among these precious pastoral couples in Cuba for approximately three weeks each visit, also hearing of their joys and sorrows, one of my final messages to them was from Christ's sermon to the church in Smyrna. I explained how I could visualize Jesus speaking to them identical words to the ones He spoke to that suffering church, "I know your tribulation and your poverty, but *you are rich*" (Revelation 2:9; italics mine). While the church in Cuba will never enjoy the earthly resources most of us in the U. S. take for granted, there was a spiritual richness in their supportive fellowship that was extraordinary, a rich vibrancy all too often missing in churches in the United States.

Dietrich Bonhoeffer (1906-1945), a renowned German pastor, seminary professor, and author, was imprisoned, at times in solitary confinement, before being executed in 1945 by the Nazis because of his resistance to Hitler. His classic book on fellowship, entitled *Life Together,* was written during the Nazi regime while he shared the common life with 25 vicars in emergency housing in the unique fellowship of an underground seminary. In that book, Bonhoeffer compellingly addresses how highly we as believers ought to prize *true koinonia.* "It is easily forgotten that the fellowship of Christian brethren is a gift of grace, a gift of the kingdom of God that could any day be taken from us; that the time that still separates us from utter loneliness may be brief indeed. Therefore, let him who until now has had the privilege of living a common Christian life with other Christians praise God's grace from the bottom of his heart. Let him thank God on his knees and declare, it is grace, nothing but grace, that we can live in Christian community with other Christian believers."[9]

One of my ongoing prayers is that Christians in America would come to cherish fellowship this highly. As I write these words, like most of the rest of the world, my wife and I are sheltered at home because of the Covid-19 pandemic, which is being followed by dangerous, destructive protests in the major cities of our nation. Hostility is also being expressed toward the church, more than I have witnessed in my lifetime. Just how this will impact our lives, our families, and our churches in the months and years ahead is unknown. But it could be that days are coming when many of the freedoms and amenities we take for granted will no longer be available; perhaps the time will come when we in America will be persecuted for our faith. Should that happen, we may find ourselves, out of necessity, coming to treasure fellowship as highly as Dietrich Bonhoeffer articulated so passionately.

As was his intent in *Life Together,* Bonhoeffer was able to succinctly capture in his title the essence of New Testament Fellowship. Interestingly, the Greek word for church is *ekklesia,* meaning *called out ones.* This meaning is a permanent reminder that not one of us comes to Christ of our initiative. But as God calls us to

Himself, inherent in His call is a summons to community, to *life together* with other believers. No Christian is an only child; in God's design, each one of us has a family of brothers and sisters, each one redeemed and called to share the common life. New Testament fellowship is woven into the very fabric of redemption.

Various metaphors for the church are used in the New Testament epistles, each one depicting how we are to view our *life together*: Family, Bride, Vineyard, Temple, Kingdom, and Flock, but more specifically, the Body. While the other metaphors have Old Testament counterparts, the one of the Body does not. It is highly prominent, however, in the New Testament, especially in Romans, I Corinthians, and Ephesians. By seeing the church as the Body of Christ in the world, the first-century believers came to understand that despite their vast diversity, they were eternally connected to one another - joint members of the one Body of Christ.

Before we leave this initial chapter, let me give you a few glimpses of the church as the body of Christ. The first comes from Paul's words to the church in Corinth: "For by one Spirit we were all baptized into one body, whether Jews or Greeks, whether slaves or free, and we were all made to drink of one Spirit" (I Corinthians 12:13). The MacArthur Study Bible explains: "The church, the spiritual body of Christ, is formed as believers are immersed by Christ with the Holy Spirit. Christ is the baptizer who immerses each believer with the Spirit into unity with all other believers. The baptism of the Spirit is not an experience to seek, but a reality to acknowledge."[10] The Apostle Paul states that this holds true for all Christians. From the moment of salvation, the Holy Spirit comes to indwell all believers, and at that time we also become full members of Christ's body, baptized by the Spirit into Christ's church.

A second example is from Paul's letter to the church in Rome: "For just as we have many members in one body and all the members do not have the same function, so we, who are many, are one body in Christ, and *individually members one of the other*" (Romans 12:4-5; italics mine). We not only belong to Christ; we are inseparably and eternally linked as *members of one another.* We may not feel or conduct ourselves as if this were true, but this is how God sees us; He is the one who made it so. Membership in the church is a corollary of our faith in Christ.

A third and more fully developed illustration of the church as the body is in I Corinthians 12. Here Paul humorously visualizes speaking body parts to address two unbiblical attitudes, both of which work against the health and unity of Christ's church.

The initial one is *a member who does not believe or feel that he belongs to the Body.* "If the foot says, 'Because I am not a hand, I am not a part of the body,' it is not for this reason any the less a part of the body. And if the ear says, 'Because I am not an eye, I am not a part of the body,' it is not for this reason any the less a part of the body. If the whole body were an eye, where would the hearing be? If the whole body were hearing, where would the sense of smell be? But now God has placed the members, each one of them, in the body, just as He desired. If they were all one member, where would the body be? But now there are many members, but *one body*" (I Corinthians 12:15-20). In these verses, Paul uses the fascinating anatomy of the human body, a body *fearfully and wonderfully made* by God Himself. His purpose is to correct the flawed thinking of the Christian who incorrectly concludes that he or she does not belong to the spiritual Body of Christ, also designed by God. God's Word says that every member belongs, and His Word settles all disputes.

The Apostle Paul immediately moves to a second unbiblical attitude that also works against the unity and health of Christ's church: *a functioning member of the Body of Christ who does not value another member of the church, conveying the attitude that he is not needed.* "And the eye cannot say to the hand, 'I have no need of you'; or again the head to the feet, 'I have no need of you.' On the contrary, it is much truer that the members of the body which seem to be weaker are necessary; and those members of the body which we deem less honorable, on these we bestow more abundant honor, and our less presentable members become much more presentable, whereas our more presentable members have no need of it. But God has so composed the body, giving more abundant honor to that member which lacked, so that there may be no division in the body, but that the members may have the same care for one another. And if one member suffers, all the members suffer with it; if one member is honored, all the members rejoice with it. Now you are Christ's body, and individually members of it" (I Corinthians 12:21-27).

Paul's corrective illustration explains how God designed the human body in such a way that even parts that are not attractive, and rarely thought about, are more important than those which are visible to others. He also explains that the body is designed so that if one part is unhealthy and in pain, this impacts the entire body – every other part - to such an extent that they suffer as well. His response provides us with one of the most beautiful pictures in all of Scripture of the Body of Christ. His point is that each member is meant to highly value each of the other parts and never consider them unnecessary. Here again, we see a recurring emphasis on unity in verse 25, "that there may be *no division* in the body."

Paul continues by providing this attractive picture of what it means *to experience the church* in verse 26: "And if one member suffers, all the members suffer with it; if one member is honored, all the members rejoice with it." The point is that no one is to be excluded or devalued, and no one is to be left to rejoice alone.

In the chapters ahead we will see how this mutually supportive fellowship is captured in the *one another* commands found in the New Testament, primarily in the Epistles. We will also discover how these admonitions have their roots in the three-year ministry Jesus had with His disciples and in His new commandment which He gave to His apostles during their final Passover meal together.

Chapter One Discussion Questions

1. In what way is fellowship a spiritual necessity and vital to our spiritual health as believers?
2. Jerry Bridges observed that the early church "didn't just have fellowship; they devoted themselves to it." What are some tangible ways to devote ourselves to fellowship?
3. Three factors were mentioned that work against true fellowship. Do you agree with this assessment? Are there other hindrances that you see?
4. In what ways does our vertical fellowship with God impact our horizontal fellowship with one another?
5. Read Romans 1:11-12 and tell of a Christian relationship you have that is similar in quality to this?
6. Read again Dietrich Bonhoeffer's quote on the fellowship on page 17 where he describes fellowship as "a gift of grace" for which we ought "to fall on our knees and give thanks." What is your response to his description?
7. How has your understanding of fellowship expanded because of reading this chapter? Are there personal applications you believe God wants you to make as a result?

Chapter Two

The New Commandment

"A new commandment I give to you, that you love one another, even as I have loved you, that you also love one another. By this all men will know that you are My disciples, if you have love for one another."

John 13:34-35

As we read carefully through the pages of the New Testament, especially in the letters addressed to the churches, we see the authors instructing believers to engage in a myriad of activities designed for the relational health of the body. A unique word often used to describe these mutual and reciprocal actions is the Greek word *allelon.* While only one word in Greek, two words are required to translate it into English - *one another.* This distinct Greek word is used 100 times in 94 verses in the New Testament. In 58 of these, *allelon* takes the form of a command, 40 of them in the Epistles. Not surprisingly, the most common of these commands is *love one another,* found 16 times: 5 of them in John's gospel and 11 in the Epistles.

In studying the gospel accounts of Jesus' life and ministry, I have often asked myself, *Why did the twelve He chose as apostles leave everything behind to follow Him?* While they would have been captivated by the unique authority of His teaching and enthralled by His compassionate, extraordinary miracles, what I have come to understand is that it was His love that ultimately captured their hearts. The unwavering devotion Jesus gave to them over a three year period far surpassed any love they had ever known. It was so unique that a new word was required to describe it, the word *agape*, a love which has its origin in the very character of God, for *"God is love"* (I John 4:8; italics mine). These men chosen by Jesus were blessed to experience what the Apostle Paul would later describe in prayer as "the breadth and length and height and depth…and the love of Christ which surpasses knowledge" (Ephesians 3:18-19). Jesus' love was selfless, faithful, sacrificial, deliberate, and unconditional, and they were chosen to be the recipients of it in an up-close, relational way during the three years following His initial call to follow Him.

In reflecting on that extended period Jesus spent with the Twelve, Gene Getz writes, "Christ had already demonstrated His love for them. Choosing them, teaching them, protecting them, and meeting their needs were all reflections of His love. Just the fact that He made Himself nothing…being made in human likeness, and how He walked and talked with these men, was one of the greatest acts of love yet known in the universe."[1] Even with these memories permanently imbedded in their minds, it was during their last Passover meal where they would see His love expressed extraordinarily, in a way they had not yet witnessed before the cross. The Apostle John summarized that memorable evening with these words, "Having loved His own who were in the world, He loved them to the end - to the fullest possible extent" (John 13:1).

In the hours leading up to that final Passover, Jesus asked Peter and John to prepare for the feast they would share with Him later that evening. But as the disciples were on the way to that momentous gathering, "there arose also a dispute among them as to which one of them was regarded to be greatest" (Luke 22:24). Perhaps it was their argument that led to one important detail being overlooked; they failed to arrange for a servant whose task it would be to wash the feet of everyone present. As Dr. Merrill Tenney writes, "They were ready to fight for a throne but not for a towel."[2]

It was during that Passover meal when Jesus demonstrated the full extent of His love. To the shock and bewilderment of the entire group, Jesus "got up from supper, and laid aside His garments; and taking a towel, He girded Himself. Then He poured water into the basin, and began to wash the disciples' feet and to wipe them with the towel with which He was girded" (John 13:4-5). When He was finished, Jesus explained, "If I then, the Lord and the Teacher, washed your feet, you also ought to wash one another's feet. For I gave you an example that you should do as I did to you" (John 13:14-15). Just as He had served them, they would soon learn in greater detail how their call would be to "through love serve one another" (Galatians 5:13).

Later that evening Jesus went on to declare, "A new commandment I give to you, that you love one another, even as I have loved you, that you also love one another. By this all men will know that you are My disciples, if you have love for one another" (John 13:34-35). What strikes me about this remarkable moment is how there is not the slightest hint of any of His disciples asking Him to refresh their memory as to how He had loved them. Running through their minds were countless examples of how He, at every turn and in every circumstance, had given them nothing but unconditional, sacrificial love.

To grasp the impact of Jesus' new commandment, we must remember that the command to love was not new. These Jewish young men would have known by heart the *Shema*, the passage from Deuteronomy recited twice daily in devout Jewish homes: "Hear, O Israel! The Lord is our God, the Lord is one! You shall love the Lord your God with all your heart and with all your soul and with all your might" (Deuteronomy 6:4-5). Faithfully reciting the *Shema* (which means *hear* in Hebrew) indelibly imprinted on their minds their unique identity as God's chosen people. It also permanently established that the foremost calling in life was to love God wholeheartedly.

The disciples also knew well the command, "You shall love your neighbor as yourself" (Leviticus 19:18). They would have remembered how Jesus identified these two commandments, the first vertical, and the second horizontal, as the greatest of all. To love your neighbor as you love yourself had also been beautifully summarized by Jesus in words we commonly refer to as the Golden Rule: "In everything, therefore, treat people the same way you want them to treat you, for this is the Law and the Prophets" (Matthew 7:12). A legitimate question one might ask is: Why was Jesus giving them a *new commandment?* In what way was His *new commandment* different from the two He had already identified as the greatest?

In the first place, while Jesus was not annulling the command of Leviticus 19:18, He was raising the bar. Instead of the Golden Rule standard, which is unquestionably a wonderful way to live, Jesus was giving His followers a higher standard of loving, a different pattern, and example. Now they were to love one another with the same love they had received from Him during the three years they were blessed to spend in His presence. To love one another as we love ourselves was no longer the ultimate standard; in the New Commandment, Christ's love superseded it!

The second difference in Christ's new commandment is this: As those blessed to live under the new covenant, this Christ-like love would be produced, not by one's own strength, but by the Holy Spirit who would come to indwell His disciples on the Day of Pentecost. Jesus declared to them later that evening, "If you love Me, you will keep My commandments. I will ask the Father, and He will give you another Helper, that He may be with you forever...He abides with you and will be in you" (John 14:15-17). This would be the first of four succinct but compelling teachings He would give during that Passover evening about the Holy Spirit who would soon come to indwell them. We know from the New Testament that the Holy Spirit also comes to reside in all who believe, providing each one with an ability to love at the higher level of the New Commandment.

As those who desire to be obedient to His commands, which includes seeking to follow His new commandment, we are blessed with the empowerment to love. In his letter to the church at Rome, the Apostle Paul wrote that "the love of God has been poured out within our hearts through the Holy Spirit who was given to us" (Romans 5:5). When describing the fruit of the Spirit to the churches of Galatia, Paul also began with love: "But the fruit of the Spirit is love..." (Galatians 5:22). While the fruit of the Spirit totals nine in number, the initial one mentioned is love.

As a pastor of more than 50 years, as well as a husband, father, grandfather, and now great-grandfather, I have cried out to God on numerous occasions, asking Him to enable me to love when my strength to do so was depleted. Thankfully, God has answered. At times, the answer came after I had failed by attempting to love in my own strength, but the good news is that He gives the power to love to each of His children.

The third feature of Jesus' new commandment is how He gave to them the definitive mark by which they and every individual believer in His church would be known: "By this all men will know that you are My disciples, if you have love for one another" (John 13:35). His compelling charge applies to the church in every location, in every culture, and all generations, until Jesus returns to take His bride home with Him to live eternally.

Gene Getz points out that the circumstances in which Jesus' words were spoken were anything but ideal: "Think of it. Jesus Christ was about to die for the sins of the world, and His disciples – at that very moment of the Passover feast – were vying for His attention and seeking to put one another down. Jesus Christ knew all about their weaknesses, their selfish motives, and their lack of love for one another, but He loved them just the same."[3] It was to this struggling group of disciples, and to every diverse group that would follow, that Jesus made known His new commandment: "By this all men will know that you are My disciples, if you have love for one another" (John 13:35).

In reflecting on the unique mark Jesus gave, I have at times surmised about other identifying marks He could have given, such as doctrinal purity, faithful church attendance, a daily quiet time, being part of a Bible study, deeds of charity, etc. But as we know, immediately after issuing His new commandment, Jesus went on to state unequivocally that their definitive mark would be loving one another with Christlike love. We may ask - how well did this immature and somewhat divided group of disciples do in this regard?

One significant fact we know is that later that evening Jesus prayed for them: for their protection, their future ministry, but especially for their unity. "I am no longer in the world; and yet they themselves are in the world, and I come to You. Holy Father, keep them in Your name, the name which You have given Me, *that they may be one even as We are*" (John 17:11; italics mine). Later in His prayer, as He looked ahead to intercede for all who would believe on Him as a result of their ministry, Jesus again prayed for unity: "The glory which You have given Me I have given to them, *that they may be one, just as We are one; I in them and You in Me, that they may be perfected in unity,* so that the world may know that You sent Me, and loved them, even as You have loved Me" (John 17:22-23).

Significantly, Jesus linked His prayer for unity, including the love of His followers for one another, as conditions for the world knowing He was sent by the Father and that the Father loved them even as He loved His beloved Son. Francis Schaeffer refers to this as *the final apologetic,* in the sense of it being proof that we belong to Christ, but if we are without it, the world has a right to conclude that we are not true Christians. Here Jesus is stating something else which is more cutting, much more profound: we cannot expect the world

28

to believe that the Father sent the Son, that Jesus' claims are true, or that Christianity is genuine unless the world sees the reality of this oneness in true Christians."[4] Christlike love is the decisive, definitive mark of the Christian, and much is at stake.

One of the most profound comments made regarding the relational health of the first-century church came from the lips of a man named Aristides, sent by Emperor Hadrian to spy out those strange creatures known as *Christians*. Having seen them in action, Aristides returned with a mixed report. But his immortal summary to the emperor has echoed down through church history, essentially declaring, "Behold! How they love one another!"[5]

Sadly, this has not always been the case. Instead of loving one another as Christ loved, the church has far too frequently displayed to the world what some have referred to as *Christian ugliness*. It is ugly because it comes from the very ones Jesus said were to be conspicuously known by their Christlike love for one another.

Christian ugliness takes many shameful forms: apathy, arrogance, harsh critical words, insensitivity, gossip, prejudice, favoritism, hypocrisy, a divisive spirit, and many others. When this happens, the church suffers greatly. Even more, the name of Jesus is belittled and betrayed. Instead of the world being drawn to our loving Savior and Lord, the *ugliness* of His children pushes unbelievers away, leaving many disillusioned, even questioning the veracity of the Christian faith.

Though I have read many books over the years, one that has touched my life and influenced my ministry as deeply as any other is Francis Schaeffer's small booklet entitled, *The Mark of the Christian*. I have purchased copies on several occasions to give to fellow pastors, elders, staff members, and individuals with whom I was meeting in a discipleship relationship.

As God has worked in my life, both through His Word and by His Spirit about these truths, my wife and I have progressively sought to make relationships a high priority in our lives. This comes more easily for Linda because of the beautiful relational model she witnessed in her missionary parents while growing up in Medellin, Colombia. As a first-generation Christian from the hills of Appalachia, it has not come as easily for me. What has convinced me, however, in my years of studying the New Testament, is that healthy relationships are at the epicenter of a Christian perspective on life, with a Christlike love for others being the definitive mark!

The prominence of love in the New Testament Epistles gives indisputable evidence that the early church embraced *agape* love as their chief identifying mark. In I Corinthians, for example, love is described as "the more excellent way...the greatest of all the enduring qualities...and the preeminent quality we are to pursue." (See I Corinthians 12:31;13, and 14:1) In the book of Ephesians we are admonished to "Be imitators of God, as beloved children; and *walk in love*, just as Christ also loved you, and gave Himself up for us" (Ephesians 5:1-2; italics mine). In Colossians, we are instructed, "Beyond all these things put on love, which is the perfect bond of unity" (Colossians 3:14). In I Peter, we are told, "Above all, keep fervent in your love for one another, because love covers a multitude of sins" (I Peter 4:8). The Apostle John, the *Son of Thunder,* who later came to be known as the *Apostle of Love*, emphasizes this quality throughout his first epistle. One example is this: "We love, because He first loved us. If someone says, 'I love God,' and hates his brother, he is a liar; for the one who does not love his brother whom he has seen, cannot love God whom he has not seen. And this commandment we have from Him, that the one who loves God should love his brother also" (I John 4:19-21). It is clear from John's words that the new commandment of His beloved Lord was foremost in mind as he wrote.

My concern for many years, one I have often expressed in sermons, classes, and various articles, is for Christians to catch a vision of the paramount significance of our Lord's Great Commandment. We would all agree that the world deserves more from the church than *Christian ugliness*!

As I mentioned in the preface, the truths in this book first began to penetrate my heart in the early 1970s as I was reading some material on the New Testament *one another's*, given by a friend from his class at Dallas Seminary, taught by Dr. Gene Getz. That same Christian brother informed me a couple of years later that these and other related truths had been published by Dr. Getz in *Sharpening the Focus of the Church.* One statement in that enlightening book immediately captured my attention: "The evangelical church, in general, has for many years neglected the importance of relational Christianity. We have come to rely upon the 'preacher' and the 'pastor' to do 'the work of the ministry.' And on the other hand, many Christian leaders have been content to 'preach and teach' and allow the members of their congregation to sit and listen."[6]

In my ministry as a pastor, I was one who loved to *preach and teach;* the feedback I received was that most in my congregation who *sat and listened* responded positively to this way of operating. But through the study of God's Word and the biblical insights of others I respected, I began to catch a vision of relational Christianity in the New Testament. I saw that more was needed for the health of the church than faithfully gathering for preaching and teaching, as essential as that was, is, and always will be.

One conscientious student did an illuminating study on the content of the New Testament Epistles. His goal was to discover how much space was devoted to various topics, such as prayer, evangelism, spiritual growth, godliness, spiritual gifts, etc. The most fascinating highlight of his research: He found 44% of the content in the epistles is devoted to how we as followers of Christ are to relate to one another, more space than devoted to any other one topic. Only 4%, for example, is devoted to spiritual gifts. Though I have not been able to remember the person who relayed this information, as I have read through the epistles with his percentage in mind, I find no reason to question his conclusion. Think about it – 44% of the content is devoted to how we as believers are to relate to one another! I believe this deserves, as we often see in the Book of Psalms, a *Selah*, which means – *pause and think deeply about that!*

In addition, what I gradually discovered was that fulfilling Jesus' new commandment and relating to one another in New Testament fellowship is not likely to happen with people sitting in pews or rows of chairs, nor does it happen in large groups. A smaller, more intimate setting is needed where believers can safely gather, such as in the family room of a home. Gathering in this way allows church members to exercise the often lost art of hospitality. It also enables believers to comfortably interact around a portion of Scripture and then open their hearts about how it applies to their lives. When this is done in a safe and supportive atmosphere, one which includes praying for one another, we take a major step toward discovering what it means to love one another with Christlike love. We may also get a taste of New Testament fellowship (*koinonia*) in the process.

That being said, my thesis in this book is that the 58 *one another* commands in the epistles are instructive illustrations of how to love one another in the same way Jesus loved His disciples. Several of one another admonitions even state that the activity being commanded is the replication of how Jesus loved.

Here are a few examples: "Accept one another, just as Christ also accepted us to the glory of God" (Romans 15:7). "Be kind to one another, tender-hearted, forgiving each other, just as God in Christ also has forgiven you" (Ephesians 4:32). The Apostle John summarized this overarching principle: "We know love by this, that He laid down His life for us; and we ought to lay down our lives for the brethren" (I John 3:16). Simply stated, the supreme relational principle we see in the New Testament is to treat one another the way Jesus treats us.

As you begin to conscientiously engage with other believers in the *one another* admonitions, you will soon find yourself on the road to rediscovering and experiencing true *koinonia* - New Testament fellowship. Again, this will never happen with any great depth merely by attending church on Sunday morning; the answer is to purposefully become involved with a small group in *embracing* the *one another* commands – with love at the center! This is when you will begin to *experience the church.*

Most healthy churches have small groups designed for this purpose. In the previous churches where I have served, we referred to them as Flocks and then later as Life Groups. In our current church in California, we call them Shepherding Groups. Simply being in a small group does not guarantee that the level of relationships I have been describing will occur. The starting point is to have a leader with a vision for these relational dynamics, along with a group that also embraces this vision.

Finally, regardless of what the New Testament *one another* action may be, each *one another* is meant to be done in love and as an expression of love. We must keep foremost in our thinking that love is the definitive mark Jesus gave by which others will know that we are His disciples. The Apostle Paul summarizes it perfectly: "Let all that you do be done in love" (I Corinthians 16:14).

Chapter Two Discussion Questions

1. What do the words *mutual* and *reciprocal* convey about the one another's and the relational health of the church?
2. How are we to view Jesus' new commandment when compared to His earlier statement about the two commandments He identified as the greatest?
3. With the great need for Christians to be known by the definitive mark of love, what are some of the changes that need to occur for the church to pursue this with excellence?
4. What does God's Word say about the power source for loving one another as Christ has loved us? How do we tap into this power supply?
5. What makes *Christian ugliness* so ugly? What are some things we can do to avoid being ugly Christians?
6. What are some practical steps we can take to make relationships a higher priority in our lives?
7. According to the author, what is the source or origin of the one another's? Where was this type of relating first observed in the New Testament?
8. Describe a time in the church when you were the recipient of Christlike love.

Chapter Three
Greet One Another

"Greet one another with a holy kiss."

Romans 16:16

Anytime I have presented this intriguing *one another* command in a sermon or Sunday school class, people lightheartedly express apprehension, especially as they speculate about what my application might be.

What many fail to realize is that this oft-overlooked command to *greet one another with a holy kiss* is included four times by the Apostle Paul in his epistles: Romans 16:16; I Corinthians 16:20; II Corinthians 13:12, and I Thessalonians 5:26. In each case, it comes near the end of his letter. In Romans, Paul goes on to greet 26 people by name, in each instance including some affirming word or expression of thanks.

The Apostle Peter has essentially the same command, also near the conclusion of his first epistle, but with a slight variation, "Greet one another with a kiss of love" (I Peter 5:14). In Peter's case, as John Piper points out, "Peter was writing to a persecuted, beleaguered church, seeking to encourage them on how to live as exiles in a vast sea of unbelievers who were being hostile to them. And he is laboring to help them not just show dutiful, sacrificial love to each other, but rather to feel earnest, heartfelt affection for one another."[1] This helps explain why Peter concluded by admonishing them to "greet one another with a kiss of love." He was calling for the church to be more purposeful in how they approached and greeted one another, so that each one could be renewed and refreshed to face the challenges of living amid an increasingly hostile world.

Note that in all five references, each command has three parts: the first is the action commanded – *to greet*. The second is the form the greeting was to take – *with a kiss*. The third highlights the moral excellence of the greeting – it was to be *holy or expressed in love.*

As we reflect on how this *one another* command applies to our gatherings today, we easily recognize that the form of this holy greeting of love is determined primarily by culture. In New Testament times it was obviously with a kiss, but the form the greeting takes can vary considerably from one culture to another.

In America, our most common church greeting is a simple good morning, good afternoon, or good evening, often accompanied by a warm handshake. Depending on the nature of the relationship, it may at times include an affectionate hug.

Christian greetings vary greatly in the diverse cultures of the world. In our two memorable visits among the Christians in Japan, for example, their way of greeting is a polite and respectful bow, and often more than one is given. The Christian men of the Ketengban tribal group in Papua, Indonesia, where we have visited linguists and Bible translation friends on two occasions, have what could best be referred to a *knuckle pop*, often a loud exchange that requires both strength and skill. Among the Mixteco people in the mountains of Oaxaca, they have a light handshake, but not as strong as we are accustomed to in America. It is very deliberate, however, and each person gives this gesture to everyone present, both young and old, upon arrival and again on departure.

My closest experience to the *holy kiss* or *kiss of love* came during our visits to Cuba in 2010. Among the Christians, the form of the greeting often included a *holy kiss*, at least from the women to me as a visiting pastor. Even the tiniest girls would wait for me to bend over so they could give me a light kiss on the cheek. Upon our return to the U.S., I commented that I had never been kissed by so many unknown women in my life, but I liked it and felt honored. To them, it was a *holy kiss*, a *kiss of love* that was given to me, a pastor, as an expression of respect and gratitude.

The question I want to set forth is this: What is it that makes a greeting distinctively Christian? What makes it holy? What is it that elevates this greeting above the culture to be a genuine expression of Christian love? One thing we know is that the answer is not in the form.

From my study of God's Word and my reflection on the greetings I have observed among believers in various cultures, I have reached this conclusion: *A greeting is distinctively Christian when one believer lovingly acknowledges another believer for who he or she is in the Lord, whether by attitude, by actions, by words, or by all three. For a greeting to be truly Christian there must be sincere warmth and affection based on the truth that all followers of Christ share a bond in Him that is deeply spiritual, one that will last throughout eternity.*

As we prayerfully reflect on ways to integrate this *one another* truth into our lives, there are two areas of application to consider. The first is how we greet the newer people, those unknown to us, who come among us when the church is gathering.

Can you remember being in the position of a first-time visitor to a church? Being a pastor, the only occasions when my wife and I have this experience is on vacation. Even then, we often are visiting family, meaning that people in their church know who we are and feel obligated to greet us warmly.

Some years ago, however, we had the opportunity to be regular visitors. Our church in Indianapolis gave me time away for a three-month sabbatical. We were blessed to spend it in Ft. Myers, Florida, on the 8th floor of a gorgeous condominium with a perfect view of the Gulf of Mexico, the bridge to Sanibel Island, and stunning sunsets every evening. It was generously made available to us by loyal friends in our church.

Because sincerely greeting the new people who come among us is something I highly value and often stress to our church family, I was interested to see how friendly the Ft. Myers churches would be as we came among them as visitors during the weeks of my sabbatical. Sadly, other than a designated greeter or the usher who handed us a bulletin, we were largely ignored in the churches we visited. While there is certainly more to church health than how they greet their visitors (or guests, as I prefer to call them), a church has only one opportunity to make a first impression. My passion as a pastor is to see that the initial greeting be one of genuine love. Let me suggest some ways we can make it this.

First, *warmly greeting the guests who come among us is an opportunity to express Christian hospitality.* I contend that we should treat our church guests the same as if we had invited them into our home. Our church facility in a very real sense is our residence; as members, we are hosts and hostesses whose responsibility it is to warmly greet our guests, showing them the same level of Christian hospitality we would if they came into our private home.

Alexander Strauch, in his excellent book, *The Hospitality Commands,* makes the point that Christian hospitality is meant to take place in the context of brotherly love and is an expression of it.[2] The writer of Hebrews makes this clear: "Let love of the brethren continue. Do not neglect to show hospitality to strangers, for by this some have entertained angels without knowing it" (Hebrews 13:1-2). Even if the guest we greet is not an angel, he or she could in time become one of our absolute best friends and a wonderful addition to our church family.

Second, *warmly greeting our guests provides a perfect opportunity to apply Jesus' golden rule*: "In everything, therefore, treat people the same way you want them to treat you" (Matthew 7:12). While Jesus never referred to His words with this designation, others have done so because it is such an instructive relational principle – a discerning, sensitive way to express love.

There is so much God can teach us when we seek to put ourselves in the position of the other person. God once spoke to the prophet Ezekiel, instructing him to go and sit in sacramental silence among a group of captives for seven days, so that he might better identify with their suffering, and he benefited (Ezekiel 3:13-14). God also gave this identical principle to His people soon after the Exodus: "You shall not despise the stranger, since you yourselves know the feelings of a stranger, for you also were strangers in the land of Egypt" (Exodus 23:9). If we could recall what our feelings were when we first came as outsiders to a church and then treat those who are new the way we would love to have been treated, our greeting will always be of much higher quality.

Third, *warmly greeting our guests provides a wonderful opportunity to join God as His fellow worker*. On at least two occasions in the New Testament, this extraordinary truth is highlighted. The first is when the Apostle Paul simply states, "We are God's fellow-workers" (I Corinthians 3:9). In his second letter to Corinth, Paul again writes, "And working together with Him, we also urge you not to receive the grace of God in vain" (II Corinthians 6:1). In his well-known book, *Experiencing God*, Henry Blackaby speaks of how this applies: *"Be alert to see how God is at work, and then join Him."*[3]

When new people come among us as guests, we have no way of knowing where that person is in his or her relationship with God.

The fact that they are coming likely indicates that God is already at work within them in some way. Perhaps our unknown guest is an unbeliever God is in the process of calling to Himself. Our guest could also be a new believer who needs encouragement and searching for a church family where he can grow. It could also be that our guest is a wounded believer seeking to find their way home or even a mature believer who will one day add immeasurably to the life and ministry of our church. Regardless of where our unknown guests may be spiritually, we have the lofty privilege of joining God as His fellow-workers – partnering with Him in His eternal work!

One of my favorite biblical examples of this is when a suspicious newcomer by the name of Saul of Tarsus came to visit the church: "When he came to Jerusalem, he was trying to associate with the disciples; but they were all afraid of him, not believing that he was a disciple" (Acts 9:26). With Saul having been the number one enemy of the church, the man who had arrested and persecuted Christians, we can certainly understand the fear of those in the church. But, as the book of Acts carefully documents, there was one person available to become God's fellow-worker. "But Barnabas took hold of him and brought him to the apostles and described to them how he had seen the Lord on the road, and that He had talked to him, and how at Damascus he had spoken out boldly in the name of Jesus. And he was with them, moving about freely in Jerusalem, speaking out boldly in the name of the Lord" (Acts 9:27-28). In God's sovereignty, Barnabas also became a faithful, ongoing encourager to him over several years, enabling Saul to transition into his ministry as the Apostle Paul, who would take the Gospel of Christ to the Gentile world in three fruitful missionary journeys, followed by a trip to Rome.

In our church in Porterville, we had a precious lady by the name of Orlanda, who is now with the Lord. One of her greatest contributions was the passion she displayed in warmly greeting anyone new to our church. While this is one of my passions as well,

Orlanda would often check to make sure I had greeted and met the new people who were among us that Sunday. As one example, some friends of ours came to visit one morning from a nearby community, sensing that God was leading them to find a new church home. Like clockwork, Orlanda immediately met and welcomed our friends, who are now faithful members of the church. The wife later informed me that when they returned for a second visit, Orlanda not only remembered her name and the name of her husband, she also was able to recall the names of their three children! Every church needs an Orlanda!

Before we leave this point, I must share an unforgettable experience I had in the late 1970s when I was pastor at Grace Community Church in Tyler, Texas. One Sunday evening, as the service was beginning, I noticed two women, unknown to me, enter and take a seat in the back of the church. My thought was that they were likely mother and daughter. Since I had not been able to greet them, and it appeared no one else had spoken to them, I purposed to seek them out afterward. But when the service ended, I was delayed by a couple of people who wanted to talk. By the time I could rush outside to search for them, they were already getting into their car, ready to drive away. I quickly ran and was thankfully able to reach them before they could leave. The older one, the mother, rolled her window down so I could speak to her. As I greeted her and her daughter, after a friendly exchange the mother spoke words to me, a statement I have never forgotten. With deep emotion, she said, "We have been visiting churches for a few weeks, but not one person in any of them has spoken to us. And again tonight, no one greeted us until you came running up to our car." And then she said: *"Before we came, we had decided to give God one more chance, and now - here you are – as an answer to our prayer!"*

Had there been opportunities for Christians in the churches they visited *to show them hospitality, to practice the golden rule, and to be God's fellow-workers*? Indeed, there were, but everyone missed those opportunities, and I almost did as well. While I was able to assure this disheartened mother and daughter of God's love and offer some encouragement, her words left an indelible impression on me about the enormous significance of this ministry of greeting.

When I retired from LifePoint Church in Indianapolis in April of 2009 after 24 years, the church graciously gave us a cruise with Dr. David Jeremiah and his team. It originated in Boston, traveled north to Maine, Nova Scotia, Prince Edward Island, and down the St. Lawrence Seaway, ultimately ending in Montreal. The church also gave us two large, attractively bound books filled with pictures, notes, and letters from people in our congregation. While the cruise was wonderful, it is now an event in the distant past. The books, however, contain numerous expressions of love from those who were part of our church family over many years. One of the features that captured my attention the first time I read them, and on other occasions in the years since, is that so many referenced details of how I greeted them when they first came or how I remembered their names or sought them out to introduce myself and get to know who they were. While neither I nor our church family did it perfectly, reading their comments reinforced in me this truth: Greeting the guests who come among us is considerably more important than the casual way most in the church approach it; the effects of this ministry can be far-reaching.

The second application to the *greet one another with a holy kiss* command has to do with how we relate to the people we already know within our church family. The truths I want to highlight in this application emerge from Paul's instructive greetings in the final chapter of his letter to the church at Rome.

First, *greeting one another with Christ's love is an affirmation of the eternal relationship we share with all those who are in Christ.* In Paul's final greetings to the church in Rome, the phrase *in Christ* or its equivalent is found 9 times in the first 13 verses. This simply stated truth affirmed the intimate, eternal nature of the relationship Paul shared with the people in the church

We often speak today of Christ being in us, a truth we see in God's Word. What we may not know is that the truth of us being *in Christ* is far more prominent, occurring 172 times in the New Testament. Paul uses the phrase 97 times in his epistles, and it describes our identity as Christians, not only individually but corporately, and it is a substantial part of our eternal identity.

While this is true, the sad reality is that many Christians never come to know their brothers and sisters in Christ at this level. Part of this disparity is because we do not know one another's stories of redemption - how God graciously called us to Himself and into His family. When we take the time and provide opportunities for this to happen, there is immediately a deeper sense of bonding.

Another significant fact about the list of those *in Christ* who were greeted by Paul is their diversity. There were Jews and Gentiles; some were slaves, and others were free; some were men, and others were women; some were rich, and others were poor. What made the difference was that they were all *in Christ*. Because of His redeeming grace, "There is neither Jew nor Greek, there is neither slave nor free man, there is neither male nor female; for you are all one in Christ Jesus" (Galatians 3:28).

Second, *greeting one another with Christ's love is an expression of the unique family affection known only to God's children.*

Again, within Paul's comments in Romans 16 are numerous expressions of endearment. His greetings go beyond the small talk and the common cultural greetings even strangers give to one another. Because Paul was greeting them as an expression of brotherly love, his brief affirmations are laced with affection and memories of shared experiences in their common faith.

He speaks, for example, of Phoebe as *our sister*, of Priscilla and Aquila as *my fellow workers,* of Epaenetus as *my well beloved,* of Andronicus and Junia as *my fellow prisoners*, of Amplias as *my beloved in the Lord*, of Stachys and Persis as *my beloved*, and Rufus' mother as *his mother and mine.* While his greetings are concise, in each case he is recalling a shared experience, whether in ministry, in prison, in homes, or some other setting.

Paul's greetings remind us of the affectionate relationships many of us are blessed to share because our church involvement progressed beyond the casual Sunday morning experience. While relationships often begin in the large gatherings, they deepen in small groups and in shared ministry experiences, such as serving with others in the nursery, in children's Sunday school, youth ministry, or on the worship team.

Because of the continuing involvement Linda and I have in short term mission trips, we have witnessed the forging of deep friendships during these shared ministry experiences. Because our trips are most often intergenerational in makeup, it is not unusual to see teens serving alongside those in their 70s or 80s, with both getting a taste of true *koinonia, New Testament fellowship.* This intergenerational component is so beneficial for everyone involved. My wife and I are blessed that four of our grandchildren have been part of these teams, most on more than one occasion. While intergenerational relationships are not always possible, it is something we encourage in our small groups at the church.

Finally, *greeting one another with Christ's love is the launching point for celebrating God's ongoing work in each of our lives.* This is another truth I see in Paul's brief but insightful greetings; his comments affirmed and celebrated God's continuing work in each individual.

He spoke of Phoebe, *a servant of the church...(who) has been a great help to many, and of myself as well.* He affirmed Priscilla and

Aquilla who *for my own life risked their own necks, and to whom not only do I give thanks, but also all the churches of the Gentiles.* He commended Mary to the church because *she has worked hard for you.* He then listed Urbanus, whom he referred to as *our fellow-worker in Christ,* as well as Tryphena and Tryphosa, identified by Paul as *workers in the Lord.*

My experience is that the more we share in ministry together, becoming acquainted with one another's story of redeeming grace, along with the concerns and burdens we carry, the greater will be the spiritual quality of our greetings. While a *kiss* may not be part of our cultural greetings, each one can be an expression of *holy love.*

God-honoring relationships in the church are the result of learning to truly value each member of the church. Though some may not see themselves as vital members, God's Word tells us that if they belong to Christ, they are members of His body. For each member to participate in a healthy way, we must overcome attitudes of independence, of prideful superiority, and of self-pitying inferiority; all this begins with elevating the way we greet one another – purposing to do so with a Christlike attitude.

Chapter Three Discussion Questions

1. What was the author implying when he stated that the command to greet one another is to be done with moral excellence? How can we elevate our often shallow greetings to this higher level?
2. Read again the author's description of what makes a greeting distinctively Christian. What are some of the marks mentioned in this chapter that makes a greeting *distinctively Christian*?
3. What three ministry opportunities are mentioned when greeting guests new to our church? To what extent have you experienced one or more of these? Why was Barnabas mentioned as an example of how to greet newcomers?
4. What are some practical things we can purpose to do to elevate the way we greet one another as Christian friends?
5. Share the most memorable greeting experience you can recall, either when you were greeted or were the greeter.
6. What is one practical application sense you need to take away from this chapter?

Chapter Four

Accept One Another

"Therefore, accept one another, just as Christ also accepted us to the glory of God."

Romans 15:7

One of the most painful experiences anyone will ever endure is to be rejected, and it is likely that each one of us will experience this at some point in our lives. Interestingly, our Lord Himself lived with this throughout His ministry. Even though He was the Creator of the world, and the long-awaited, promised Messiah, He encountered rejection from the moment He arrived. "He was in the world, and the world was made through Him, and the world did not know Him. He came to His own, and those who were His own did not receive Him" (John 1:10-11).

In contrast, the good news of the Gospel of grace is that we as believers are eternally accepted in Christ. He "predestined us to adoption as sons by Jesus Christ to Himself, according to the good pleasure of His will, to the praise of the glory of His grace, by which *He made us accepted in the Beloved*" (Ephesians 1:5-6 NKJV; italics mine).[1]

It would be difficult to find words in any language more glorious than these – *He has made us accepted in Christ.* From the moment we respond in faith to God's gracious call, we are eternally accepted because of what Jesus accomplished on our behalf. Though others may reject us at various points in our lives, knowing we are accepted by God is what matters most. This magnificent possession is ours not because of anything we have done or could ever do; God

Himself brought it about, and it is appropriately - to the praise of His grace.

As mentioned in an earlier chapter, the fundamental relational principle in the New Testament is to graciously give to others what we have first received from Christ. This is also one of my chief suppositions in highlighting the instructive collection of *one another* commands we see in the Epistles. They have their beginning in our Lord Jesus Christ, specifically in how He perfectly loved His initial followers and then us as well. Our focal verse for this chapter states this explicitly: *"Accept one another, just as Christ also accepted us."* While we may have exemplary mentors throughout our lives, our supreme example is always the Lord Jesus Christ. "Christ also suffered for you, leaving you an example for you to follow in His steps" (I Peter 2:21). "The one who says he abides in Him ought himself to walk in the same manner as He walked" (I John 2:6).

In looking at that initial group of followers chosen by Jesus, each one had quirks and idiosyncrasies when He called them, and many flaws remained during their years of following Him. In grace, however, He accepted them for where they were, all while teaching them the ways of God, pouring into them His perfect life. The two fishermen brothers, James and John, were initially known as *Sons of Thunder,* once desiring to call down fire from heaven on those who did not agree with them (Luke 9:54). Peter was impetuous, often speaking without thinking and having to be corrected by Jesus (Matthew 16:22-23). Thomas was filled with questions, often expressing doubts about his faith (John 11:16). Simon the Zealot came from one of the radical political parties of the day (Luke 6:15). Even so, Jesus met each man where he was, lovingly correcting them when needed, but always in an atmosphere of complete acceptance.

One encouraging example of this came during that last Passover when Jesus said, "I have many more things to say to you, but you cannot bear them now. But when He, the Spirit of truth, comes, He will guide you into all the truth" (John 16:12-13). Even though Jesus understood that they needed considerably more of what He wanted to teach them, He also saw that they were not yet ready to receive it. Even so, He patiently accepted them for where they were while affirming His confidence in the Holy Spirit who would soon come to indwell them and finish the work He had already begun in them.

It has been and continues to be a great joy for me as a pastor to share the gospel with others. Part of my message is to let those with whom I speak know that Jesus will meet them wherever they are, without them having to make self-improvement changes before coming. He does not plan to leave them there, of course, for repentance and spiritual transformation will soon follow. But from the time He calls us to Himself, we are, as we saw earlier, *accepted in the beloved.* (Ephesians 1:6). This acceptance is not based on who we are or what we have done, but on God's sovereign grace given to us through Christ who accomplished our full redemption. As astonishing as this may seem, the central truth of this chapter is that this loving acceptance we have received in Christ is what we are called to give to one another.

The sad reality in many churches, however, is that some will never experience this level of Christlike acceptance from their fellow believers. We can rationalize and blame them for their insecurity and insensitivity, but their rejection is often due to our lack of Christlike love as a church body.

To get to the heart of what it means to accept, we turn first to the word itself. While our English word for accept has a limited number of synonyms, such as *receive* or perhaps, *take*, the Greek language is much different. While there is a root word for accept - the Greek word *lambano* – there are at least seven variations of it.

There is also another related word for accept, and it too has several shades of meaning.

Without getting too technical, the word translated *accept* in Romans 15:7 – *proslambano* – means *to take to oneself, and it always conveys a special interest on the part of the one doing the accepting.* It is the idea of a warm, gracious, sincere welcome. If we were to translate Paul's command literally, it could read as follows: *"Keep on accepting one another warmly and sincerely."*

What I often find helpful in understanding the full meaning of a word is to see how it is used other places in Scripture. In the case of accept, the relational meaning is beautifully illustrated twice in Paul's ministry connections.

The first occurs during Paul's journey to Rome as a prisoner. He had previously taken three fruitful missionary journeys, but his dream was of going to Rome. When that time finally arrived, he was being escorted as a prisoner to stand trial before Caesar. On that journey, Paul, and all those on board the ship (276 persons) were in a terrible shipwreck. (See Acts 27.) Because of God's sovereign hand on Paul's life and ministry, coupled with his trust in the Lord, Paul and every single passenger arrived safely on land, some grasping planks from the ship, and others clinging to cargo to keep themselves afloat. The shipwreck occurred just off the island of Malta, about 50 miles south of Sicily.

It was after Paul and his companions arrived on land where we see the word *accept* used. Paul's traveling companion, Luke, describes the scene: "The natives showed us extraordinary kindness; for because of the rain that had set in and because of the cold, they kindled a fire and *accepted* us all" (Acts 28:2; italics mine). This word *accept* is identical to the word used in Romans 15:7. Note especially how the natives *built a fire and accepted them with extraordinary kindness.* My prayer is that we in the body of Christ can learn to accept one another with extraordinary kindness; whether that means building a fire for our friends or some other expression of love, we do it to the glory of God.

The second relational example where *accept* is used comes later from another of the Apostle Paul's ministry connections, this one in his brief postcard epistle of Philemon. Philemon was a first-century slave owner whose slave, Onesimus, ran away, fleeing to the large city of Rome. In the remarkable providence of God, he ended up in the same prison as Paul, where he came to faith in Christ. At some point after hearing his story, the Apostle appealed to Onesimus to return to his master, Philemon. The short, one-chapter book of Philemon contains Paul's delightful appeal to his friend and brother in Christ on behalf of Onesimus. Here are Paul's words: "Therefore, though I have enough confidence in Christ to order you to do what is proper, yet for love's sake I rather appeal to you – since I am such a person as Paul, the aged, and now also a prisoner of Christ Jesus – I appeal to you for my child, Onesimus, whom I have begotten in my imprisonment, who formerly was useless to you, but now is useful both to you and to me"(Philemon 8-11). As Paul continued his appeal, he wrote, "If then you regard me as a partner, *accept* him as you would me. But if he has wronged you in any way or owes you anything, charge that to my account" (Philemon 17, 18; italics mine).

In Paul's words, we again see the warmth and kindness that is linked to *acceptance*. Paul was urging Philemon to show his runaway slave, but now a believer, the same level of acceptance Philemon would give to him as his friend in Christ, and a highly esteemed apostle!

The extraordinary message in the book of Philemon reminds us that one of the attractive marks of the first-century church was how the barriers that divided people were broken down through the gospel: racial barriers, socio-economic barriers, age barriers, even the ones between masters and slaves, were all removed in Christ

51

who was the basis of their peace - they *accepted one another even as Christ had accepted them to the glory of God.*

As we return to our pivotal command in Romans 15, it is necessary to see that Paul's admonition to accept one another has its contextual roots in the opening words of the previous chapter: "Now accept the one who is weak in faith, but not for the purpose of passing judgment on his opinions" (Romans 14:1). The MacArthur Study Bible points out that "the *weak in faith* included both Jew and Gentile believers who were continuing to hold on to their past due to not yet having a full understanding of the truth. The young Jewish believers were having difficulty leaving the rites and prohibitions of the Old Covenant, continuing to feel compelled to adhere to various dietary laws, to observe the Sabbath, and even to offer sacrifices in the temple. In contrast, the Gentile believers who were still young in their faith had been steeped in pagan idolatry and its rituals, and as new, untaught believers, they believed that contact with anything remotely related to their past, especially eating meat that had been sacrificed to an idol, meant they were still participating in their old way of life."[2] Paul's command, nevertheless, was to accept them, allowing them to have time to "grow in the grace and knowledge of our Lord and Savior Jesus Christ" (II Peter 3:18).

We understand from the context that Paul's appeal - to accept those who were weak in their faith, without passing judgment on their opinions - was addressed to stronger believers who had gained a fuller understanding of the truth. The more mature Jewish believers were enjoying their freedom in Christ, knowing that the ceremonial *requirements* of the Old Testament law were no longer binding; they understood that Jesus and what He accomplished was enough! The Gentiles, whose faith was more developed, had come to understand that idols were not literally gods, and this truth gave them the freedom to eat and enjoy meat in the market, even though the food had been sacrificed to idols.

Paul strengthened his appeal to those who were more mature by asking, "Who are you to judge the servant of another? To his own master, he stands or falls; and he will stand, for the Lord is able to make him stand" (Romans 14:4). In this same context, he gave an additional *one another* command, one we will consider in a later chapter in more detail: "Therefore let us not judge one another anymore, but rather determine this – not to put an obstacle or stumbling block in a brother's way" (Romans 14:13).

Paul's irrefutable argument is this: To accept a young, immature believer who was weak in his or her faith, but who was, nevertheless, the servant of another – the *Another* being the One who is the identical Master of the more mature believer - means we are not in a position to pass judgment, because, at the most basic level of our identity, all believers are fellow-servants. Also, as those accepted by Christ, we are to show younger believers the same acceptance He has given us, to the glory of God.

This crucial command of *accepting one another* brings to the forefront another reality we see all through the New Testament; Those of us who are members of the body of Christ are at different levels when it comes to biblical understanding as well as spiritual maturity. The Apostle John, for example, writes of some who were *children*, others who were *young men,* and still others who were *fathers,* highlighting different levels of maturity (I John 2:12-14; italics mine). In his letter to the church at Corinth, Paul spoke of the *natural person* who was not yet a believer and of the *carnal person* who was in a prolonged period of spiritual infancy, only drinking the milk of the Word – not yet ready for the meat of the Word. He then contrasts them with the *spiritual person* who was healthy and growing in his or her faith (I Corinthians 1:2-13,3:3; italics mine). Similarly, the writer of Hebrews refers to some who "by this time ought to be teachers, but need someone to teach (them) the elementary principles of the oracles of God" (Hebrews 5:12).

What this means is that we must remember that each member of Christ's church is at a different level in his growth and understanding of the truth. While salvation begins with a spiritual birth (John 3:5-7), when we receive new life, each person grows in different ways and at his own pace. While we pursue the ideal, the reality is that we are called to accept those who are at vastly different points than we are, and we also need their acceptance.

A recurring point I hope to make in these pages is that relationships are to be immeasurably different in Christ's church than in the world. This is because each Christian is a new creation, a person changed on the inside through the transforming power of the gospel. One of the major changes God brings about is how we view people. "Therefore, from now on we recognize no one according to the flesh; even though we have known Christ according to the flesh, yet now we know Him in this way no longer" (II Corinthians 5:16).

As Paul was writing his corrective words to the church about to how to view people, his thoughts turned immediately to Christ, and how they and others initially saw Him only as a mere man, by what He looked like on the outside. As the prophet Isaiah, wrote, "He had no stately form or majesty that we should look upon Him, nor appearance that we should be attracted to Him" (Isaiah 53:2). When Christ came, this is exactly what occurred. But as time passed and His ministry unfolded, especially following His crucifixion, resurrection, appearances, and ascension, their eyes were opened, as Paul said, *to no longer view Him in a worldly point of view.* They saw Him even as Isaiah had also prophesied, "He was crushed for our iniquities, the chastening for our well-being fell upon Him, and by His scourging we are healed" (Isaiah 53:5).

Paul's words also remind us that there is immeasurably more to a person than what we see on the outside. As God reminded Samuel, "God sees not as man sees, for man looks at the outward appearance, but the Lord looks at the heart" (I Samuel 16:7). Since we are new creations in Christ, we must come to see every believer as a brother or sister with whom we will spend eternity. May God guard us against rejecting people because of some shallow, superficial criteria we can easily concoct in our own minds. Instead, let us purpose to not only warmly *greet* them with holiness and love, but also *accept* them with the love, grace, and the kindness of Christ.

Finally, as we return to Romans 15 where our key verse for this chapter is found, Paul concludes his lengthy appeal to the stronger, more mature believes with the example of Christ: "Now we who are strong ought to bear the weaknesses of those without strength and not just please ourselves. Each of us is to please his neighbor for his good, to his edification. For even Christ did not please Himself, because it is written, 'THE REPROACHES OF THOSE WHO REPROACHED YOU FELL ON ME'" (Romans 15:1-3). Again, Paul presents the Lord Jesus Christ as the example of how we are to accept one another.

What we see in His example is that acceptance means far more than merely tolerating or putting up with someone; it means *accepting them as gifts from our Heavenly Father.*

Let me explain: In His wonderful prayer in John 17, prayed the evening of His betrayal and arrest, there are at least 9 instances where Jesus mentions that all those who had come to believe in Him were *gifts from His Father, gifts He was deeply thankful to receive!*

In His earlier ministry, Jesus had also spoken of this identical truth: "All that the Father *gives Me* will come to Me, and the one who comes to Me I will certainly not cast out" (John 6:37). For Jesus to reject anyone who comes to Him, or not accept one who came, would be to reject a gift from His Father, which He would never do. Rather, as the natives of Malta did for Paul and his shipwrecked companions, *Jesus accepted them with extraordinary kindness!*

As this truth has progressively penetrated my heart over many years, I have asked God to enable me, like Jesus, to gratefully *accept* the people He brings into my life as gifts from Him. I can certainly *accept* my wife of 57 years as a wonderful gift. "House and wealth are an inheritance from fathers, but a prudent wife is from the Lord" (Proverbs 19:14). Linda and I can easily *accept* our children in this same way: "Behold, children are a gift of the Lord, the fruit of the womb is a reward" (Psalm 127:3). We can also accept our grandchildren and great-grandchildren as gifts from our gracious Heavenly Father. But if I am going to accept others even as Christ accepted me – *as a gift from His Father – then I must also accept others as gifts from God to me.* This means believing He has a purpose for bringing them into my life, either for what He wants to do in their lives through me or what He plans to do in my life through them, though relationships are always for mutual benefit.

The point is that our Lord's acceptance of us as gifts from His Father teaches us that we should have as our personal application, "Therefore, accept one another, just as Christ has accepted us to the glory of God" (Romans 15:7).

Chapter Four Discussion Questions

1. Describe the basis of our acceptance before God and how this impacts the way we are to relate to one another.
2. What do we learn about acceptance from the way Jesus related to His growing yet still immature disciples?
3. How is the acceptance we are called to give more than simply tolerating or putting up with one another?
4. What struggles did Philemon possibly face when Paul appealed to him to accept back his runaway slave?
5. What factors are mentioned by the author which make accepting one another more difficult? How can we overcome these issues?
6. How are Christian relationships different from what we see in the world between unbelievers? Why is there a difference in how we view people after coming to Christ as opposed to how we looked at them before?

Chapter Five
Bear One Another's Burdens

"Bear one another's burdens, and thereby fulfill the law of Christ."

Galatians 6:2

As a relatively new Christian seeking to follow God's call, I began *preaching* during my senior year of high school. The view of my pastor was essentially, *"If God has called you to preach, then preach!"* Though still a novice, I continued to receive weekend invitations to preach during my first three years of college in the country churches of Kentucky and southern Indiana. My wife, Linda, and I were married at the end of our junior year, and I became a student pastor responsible for two sermons each Sunday for the next five years, before graduating from seminary in 1968.

At some point during my fledgling ministry, I heard two statements that influenced me greatly, ones I have never forgotten. The first was this: *Speak softly; every person you meet is carrying a heavy burden.* The second was similar: *Preach to the hurting, and you will never lack for an audience, for there are two or three in every pew.*

The title of one of my earliest sermons, one I enjoyed preaching and that seemed to always bring encouragement, was entitled, *"What to do with Life's Burdens."* Even in this autumn season of life, I still enjoy preaching, teaching, and writing on this same theme. One of the reasons springs from the encouraging truths contained in God's Word about what to do with life's burdens.

A second reason I love this theme is that I have yet to meet a person who was without burdens. While they take many forms, sooner or later each one of us will face circumstances that overwhelm and weigh us down.

The inspiration for my sermon came when I discovered three verses about burdens which at first glance appear to give contradictory instruction.

- "Every man shall bear his own burden" (Galatians 6:5).[1]

- "Bear one another's burdens, and thereby fulfill the law of Christ" (Galatians 6:2).

- "Cast your burden upon the Lord and He will sustain you" (Psalm 55:22).

As I looked at these passages more carefully, I discovered that a different word for *burden* is used in each reference. This confirmed what I already knew; the Bible was not contradicting itself. Understanding the meaning of keywords in the passage is an important key to the correct interpretation, and in this case, the meanings were packed with truth.

In Galatians 6:5 – *every man shall bear his own burden* - the Greek word translated *burden* in the KJV, is rendered *load* in the NASB and ESV. It refers essentially to a soldier's pack, or to a specified load assigned to us, one that cannot be delegated. Most of us have responsibilities of this sort in our lives.

In Galatians 6:2 – *bear one another's burdens* – the Greek word describes excessive, overwhelming burdens, beyond our strength to endure, more than we can carry alone; assistance is required. We will examine this in more detail in the pages ahead.

In Psalm 55:22 – *cast your burden on the Lord* – the Hebrew word means – *the lowest pit.* Burdens of this type cannot get any heavier; it is humanly impossible to carry them alone. Even though others may attempt to assist, their support is insufficient. The weight of this type of burden is so overwhelming that our only answer is to cast it upon the Lord. Thankfully, the verse concludes with an encouraging promise – *He will sustain you.*

The command to *bear one another's burdens* - the focus of this chapter - is an appeal to come alongside a Christian brother or sister who is heavily burdened and desperately in need of assistance. Paul explains that as we assist one another with our burdens, we are *fulfilling the law of Christ.* What Paul surely had in mind was Jesus' new commandment to *love one another even in the same way He had loved.* His command to love as He loved is the *law of Christ.* Loving in this instance takes the form of bearing the burden of a fellow believer.

While I would never add to Scripture, I believe that when we are conscientiously embracing the New Testament one another's, in love, *we are fulfilling the law of Christ.* In this instance, the Apostle removes all doubt by stating this explicitly.

The word for burden in Galatians 6:2 can be used to refer to various types of difficulties, meaning that this *one another* command can be extremely broad in its application. It often refers to physical burdens, ones we carry because of inevitable health issues and medical concerns. It can also refer to emotional burdens, such as we endure following the loss of a loved one. It can include the burdens we carry because of strained or broken relationships with family members or friends. But there are also spiritual burdens, the weight or heaviness we carry in our hearts because we have sinned.

In the opening verses of Galatians 6, Paul applies this relational principle to a burden caused by a serious spiritual issue, a person under the weight and guilt of sin. "Brethren, even if anyone is caught in any trespass, you who are spiritual, restore such a one in a spirit of gentleness, each one looking to yourself, so that you too will not be tempted. Bear one another's burdens, and thereby fulfill the law of Christ" (Galatians 6:1-2).

The circumstance Paul describes is about a Christian brother or sister who is overtaken, not so much by a pre-meditated, deliberate sin, but to the type of slip a person might make on an icy road or a slippery path. Some versions use the word *trespass* or *fault* while others use the word *sin,* and all are accurate. The situation is such, however, that the person with the *burden of sin or guilt* has been somewhat surprised, with the result being that he is overwhelmed by the weight of it all and needs the loving assistance of a fellow believer.

As I have studied this passage on different occasions, Paul's warning often comes to mind, "Therefore let him who thinks he stands take heed that he does not fall" (I Corinthians 10:12). The picture in Galatians appears to be of an arrogant believer who did not think he would fall, but he did, and the consequences were devastating. Now he is *caught in this trespass.*

From my experience as a pastor, there are times when a person with a burden such as this will come seeking assistance, and other times when they will not ask for help at all. The Apostle Paul does not specify if the person has sought out help or not; what he simply tells us is that we are to "bear one another's burdens, and thereby fulfill the law of Christ" (Galatians 6:2). Much sensitivity and discernment are required if we would recognize those around us in need of a *loving burden bearer.*

The word *bear* means *to take up, to carry, to support.* In this instance, the picture is of mature believer coming alongside to share the weight of the burden so that the person is not overwhelmed by having to carry it alone.

For the most part, the church has not done a good job in this regard, likely because it is one of our more difficult *one another* responsibilities. Sometimes the church remains apathetic, doing nothing all. At other times, people in the church go to the troubled person but with a critical spirit and judgmental attitude, and more harm is done than good. The criticism leveled against the church some years back was this: *The church is the only organization that shoots its wounded.*

The teaching Paul is describing here stands in direct opposition to shooting our wounded, as we will soon see. To understand how this wonderfully instructive passage applies to us, we must look at the larger context to see what it means to *bear one another's burdens* in this way.

In the first place, *we need to be certain that the Holy Spirit is controlling our lives.* Note that Paul's instruction is addressed to "You who are spiritual." These words are a continuation of the rich, practical teaching Paul gave to the Galatians toward the end of chapter five, summarized in the verses that follow.

"The fruit of the Spirit is love, joy, peace, patience, kindness, goodness, faithfulness, gentleness, self-control; against such things there is no law. Now those who belong to Christ Jesus have crucified the flesh with its passions and desires. If we live by the Spirit, let us also walk by the Spirit. Let us not become boastful, challenging one another, envying one another" (Galatians 5:22-26).

In this wonderfully instructive passage, one which transitions into the serious matter of *bearing one another's burdens,* Paul reminds his readers of the new life they have been graciously given as the result of their spiritual birth.

Those of us who are believers remember what it was like to be dead in our trespasses and sins, and then, through a miraculous work of the Holy Spirit, to be born again. The religious leader,

Nicodemus, who came to Jesus by night, was confused as to how a person who was old could be born again. Jesus gave this profound answer: "The wind blows where it wishes and you hear the sound of it, but do not know where it comes from and where it is going; so is everyone who is born of the Spirit" (John 3:8). Jesus wanted Nicodemus to be aware that even as there are mysterious subtleties about the wind, so it is with the Spirit. Both, nevertheless, are real, and we can see the effect in tangible ways.

In the case of being born of the Spirit, Paul described the effect in terms of fruit, the fruit of the Spirit, nine attractive qualities which portray the perfect character of Christ. As the Spirit controls our lives, these nine traits will become progressively apparent in how we relate to others. The beauty is that they are appropriate in every situation, especially in *burden-bearing,* for as Paul assures the Galatians, *against such things there is no law.*

As Paul turns to this matter of *burden-bearing,* his instruction is to "You who are spiritual" (Galatians 6:1). He is not talking about where they were at some previous point, but to their spiritual status when becoming aware of a brother or sister who has been overtaken and caught in a sin. As those who have been made alive by the Spirit, and as ones who are experiencing a measure of the fruit of the Spirit, Paul now urges them to depend on the Spirit as they approach this issue of burden-bearing. He writes, "If we live by the Spirit, let us also walk by the Spirit" (Galatians 5:25). The NIV translates the last part of Paul's admonition, "Let us keep in step with the Spirit."[2] This is essential in this burden-bearing ministry.

As I have been involved at different times in coming alongside friends in the church and beyond who are overwhelmed with a spiritual burden, I have found it essential to be prayerful each step of the way, depending on the Spirit for wisdom throughout the entire process.

A second related truth comes from the context: *approach the burdened person with an attitude of gentle humility.* Note again Paul's words, "You who are spiritual, restore such a one in a spirit of gentleness, each one looking to yourself, so that you too will not be tempted" (Galatians 6:1).

One of the most decisive issues in the success of any relationship is our attitude, and this is especially true in this instance. With each person we meet, we are building either a wall or a bridge; what makes the difference is attitude. In the case of *burden-bearing,* we want to build a bridge, especially an attitude that conveys we can be trusted.

What is clear in this passage is that our attitude is to be one of *gentle humility.* It is gentle in the sense that I am treating you today the way I hope you would treat me tomorrow if the roles were reversed and I was the one who had stumbled and fallen. It is humble in the sense that I am fully aware that though I am not the one who has fallen in this instance, I know I can fall. Each one of us is vulnerable to temptation. This is because, as the Apostle Paul once revealed about himself, "I know that nothing good dwells in me, that is in my flesh" (Romans 7:18). Being aware of how far we can fall when we yield to the flesh, ceasing to depend on Christ, enables us to go to our troubled brother or sister with an attitude of gentle humility.

This quality of gentleness is not something we produce in our strength and is why it is listed among the fruit of the Spirit. Gentleness, or meekness, as it is sometimes translated, does not mean weakness, but strength under the control of the Holy Spirit. It is one of the marks of the character of Christ who once described Himself as *gentle and humble of heart.* You may recall His statement, "Take My yoke upon you and learn from Me, for I am gentle and humble in heart" (Matthew 11:29).

If we seek to be a burden bearer without this quality, the person in need will likely resist, being unwilling to fully confess the burden of his heart in a way that is necessary for forgiveness, healing, and restoration.

The third truth to keep in mind if we are to be effective *burden bearers* is that *our primary goal is to provide spiritual support and restoration.* Look again at Paul's words, "Brethren, even if anyone is caught in any trespass, you who are spiritual, *restore* such a one in a spirit of gentleness, each one looking to yourself so that you too will not be tempted" (Galatians 6:2; italics mine).

The truth I want to highlight is in the word *restore.* When we approach a brother or sister such as Paul is describing, our goal is not to expose, to embarrass, to shame, to humiliate, to judge, to condemn, or to boast in our spiritual success; our goal is to restore this person to his or her previous standing with the Lord before being overtaken by sin.

The word Paul uses to describe this goal has some enlightening word pictures associated with it. It is used, for example, in the early chapters of Matthew when Jesus was calling His initial disciples, James and John. "Going on from there, He saw two other brothers, James the son of Zebedee, and John his brother, in the boat with Zebedee their father, *mending their nets,* and He called them. (Matthew 4:21; italics mine). The phrase, *mending their nets,* meant they were restoring them to usefulness. It is the identical Greek word Paul uses in Galatians for *restoring* our fallen, wounded brother or sister to usefulness. They are sidelined temporarily because of having been ensnared by sin, but our goal as a Spirit-controlled believer is to restore them to usefulness in the body of Christ.

This same word is also used in classical Greek, and the word picture is similar. It means to *restore or reset a bone that has been broken.* It can also mean to surgically remove a diseased growth from someone's body.[3]

The intent in coming alongside a wounded Christian warrior, as expressed so clearly in Paul's instruction, is not for punishment but to provide a cure. While correction is part of the process, it is redemptive and purposeful, namely, to restore to usefulness and make one whole. When we see it in this way, the quality of gentleness is reinforced even more strongly.

In looking back over my many years of ministry and following the Lord, I am thankful for the people who have come alongside me in the way described in this passage. They were spiritual people who came with a gentle humility, Christian brothers who believed in the genuineness of God's work in my life, even when I had temporarily lost sight of it. They helped me find healing and restoration to usefulness in ministry. It is never an easy process, but the outcome is beautiful and filled with joy, as we see here.

As I mentioned earlier, when we are lovingly involved in this ministry, keeping in step with the Holy Spirit who indwells us, we are *fulfilling the law of Christ*. Even as Jesus lovingly bore the deep spiritual burdens of His initial followers, we too are called to follow His example, to walk in His steps.

"Blessed be the Lord, who daily bears our burden" (Psalm 68:19).

Chapter Five Discussion Questions

1. What are the three answers the Bible gives about what to do with life's burdens? Why do different types of burdens require different answers?
2. When you have carried a heavy burden in the past, what have others done that gave you the most help and support? What are some things that did not help?
3. While Christians have at times "shot their wounded", what are the biblical alternatives to this sad practice?
4. Look again at what the author describes as *gentle humility*, and discuss why it is gentle, and why it is humble. Why are both needed when approaching someone who has fallen.
5. Look again at the phrase "you who are spiritual" and discuss how it is linked to Paul's teaching about the Holy Spirit in chapter five. What are the key points in Paul's instruction? Why is the Holy Spirit's assistance essential in burden-bearing?
6. What can we do to be more alert to those in the church and beyond who are carrying heavy burdens and need support?

Chapter Six
Be Devoted to One Another

"Be devoted to one another in brotherly love."

Romans 12:10

One cannot spend consistent time in the New Testament without coming face to face with the reality that healthy relationships are God's will for His children. The one another truths, so skillfully woven by the Holy Spirit into the very fabric of the New Testament Epistles, give irrefutable support to this truth.

Our current one another focus comes from the twelfth chapter of Romans, one of the most enlightening relational passages in the entire New Testament. In this rich section of Scripture, we learn that whether we are relating to our brothers and sisters in Christ, or coming face to face with our worst enemies, our calling as God's children is to always display love.

Having a passion to give love stands in sharp contrast to what we typically see in today's world where most are looking out only for themselves. Without Christ, committed relationships are difficult if not impossible to establish, with most characterized by ongoing relational conflicts. To those of us, however, who have a degree of fluency with God's Word, and are progressively being transformed by the power of Christ, our motivation is to make love our aim in all relationships.

While this is unquestionably our calling, love does not come naturally for anyone. Loving is possible only because our gracious

Father reached out in love, calling us to Himself: "We love because He first loved us" (I John 4:19). In responding to His love, we discover an entirely new way of living and a superior way of loving. The Holy Spirit takes up residence in us and is the one who empowers us to love. The Apostle Paul explains, "The love of God has been poured out within our hearts through the Holy Spirit who has been given to us" (Romans 5:5).

As we learned in chapter two, this Christlike love is the definitive mark that enables a watching world to know we are true Christians. The Apostle John explains, "We know that we have passed out of death into life because we love our brothers. He who does not love abides in death" (I John 3:14). It would be difficult to state it any more clearly, but John repeatedly returns to the theme of love several times in his first epistle. His point is that if our lives are not marked by Christlike love, this gives evidence that we have not yet received spiritual life.

Each of the 58 one another's, when practiced as our Lord intends, is a unique expression of God's love. Authentic Christianity is always relational; it is love in action, but these actions take countless forms. In the one another admonition highlighted in this chapter, it is expressed through loyal devotion, such as we see in healthy families: "Be devoted to one another in brotherly love; give preference to one another in honor" (Romans 12:10).

Before we examine the specifics of this verse, looking into what it means and how it applies to our lives, it is helpful to see the larger context where the command is found.

In the opening part of the chapter, the Apostle Paul presents the church as a healthy body; in the closing section, he describes it as a healthy family. Other metaphors are also utilized throughout Scripture to describe Christ's church. In several passages, the church is described as a flock, with Jesus being the Good, Great, and Chief Shepherd. In John 15, the church is depicted by Jesus Himself as a vineyard, with Him being the Vine, His Father the Vinedresser, and believers as the branches. In other passages the church is viewed as a building, with Christ as the foundation and Chief Cornerstone, and believers the living stones within the building. In several places, it is also described as a kingdom with Jesus being the King and His followers the subjects in His kingdom. Two of the most prominent descriptions of the church, however, are the ones we see in Romans 12, the Body, and the Family.

It was five decades ago that God worked through one of the verses in this chapter to capture my heart with the value of the one another's: "We who are many are one body in Christ, *and individually members one of the other*" (Romans 12:5; italics mine). This verse assures us that every individual member of the body is essential, for it is linked to every other part. In this metaphor, each member belongs first to Christ who is the Head of His church, but collectively to every other member as well. I often refer to this as *church membership as God designed it!*

With this background, we move ahead in Romans 12 to our key verse for this chapter. In it, Paul transitions from viewing the church as a body, to seeing it as a loving, affectionate family. Gene Getz provides this insight, "The concept of a family adds a dimension of warmth, tenderness, concern and loyalty; in short, human emotion and devotion."[1] Relational Christianity at its best is a picture of a healthy family.

In making this point, I am aware that viewing the church as a family can be difficult, if not impossible for those who grew up with no other option than to endure life in highly dysfunctional homes. I have friends who were raised without the benefit of any family at all; even the mere mention of the word father can be extremely painful. In some instances, this is due to tragic abuse of one form or another. I know others who were completely abandoned by their father, a deeply distressing experience that leaves a profound wound.

On a more positive note, I have been blessed as a pastor to witness deeply wounded men and women from dysfunctional families completely transformed by coming to know God as their loving Father. Regardless of how painful their past, in coming to faith through Jesus Christ, they discover in their Heavenly Father a depth of love and sense of security no earthly father can give. Another serendipitous benefit is that many find in the church the family they always longed for and dreamed of having, but never knew existed.

One of the passages describing this grand truth is in Paul's prayer for the church at Ephesus: "For this reason, I bow my knees before the Father, from whom every family in heaven and on earth derives its name" (Ephesians 3:14-15). After reminding them that Christ dwells in their hearts by faith, Paul goes on to ask that they, being "rooted and grounded in love, may be able to comprehend with all the saints what is the breadth and length and height and depth, and to know the love of Christ which surpasses knowledge" (Ephesians 3:18-19).

When our children were younger, we taught them I Corinthians 13, the classic chapter on *agape* love in the New Testament. We chose to have them learn it from The Living Bible, a paraphrase by Kenneth Taylor, who wrote it as a labor of love to help his children better understand God's Word. We and our children memorized these words: "If you love someone, you will be loyal to him no matter what the cost. You will always believe in him, always expect the best of him, and always stand your ground in defending him" (I Corinthians 13:7 TLB[2]). What an incredible picture of loyal, devoted love!

As we move to our key verse for the chapter, one which speaks of brotherly love, it is helpful to know that the term *brothers* is used to refer to the Christian family 230 times in the New Testament, beginning in the Book of Acts, and continuing through the epistles. In addition to Paul, the term is used by Luke, James,

John, and Peter. Gene Getz again comments, "The word *brothers* literally means 'from the same womb.' It is distinctly a family term. When it refers to Christians, it means 'fellow believers,' 'members of God's family,' 'brothers and sisters in Christ.' It means we have all been born again into God's forever family. We are vitally related to one another in a common heritage."[3]

In terms of application, our Lord never intended for His church to be simply a collection of acquaintances, or gathering of friends; He made us a family - His family! As we meet each Lord's Day, how wonderful it would be if we could view each gathering as *a mini family reunion!* The church is a redeemed, grateful family gathering to worship our Father, through His Son, Jesus Christ, in the power of the Holy Spirit who lives within each one of us.

In the paragraph where our key verse is found, Paul's opening statement is an appeal for authentic, *agape* love, the word used most often in his letter to the church at Rome. *Agape* is the primary word for love in the New Testament. The statement simply reads, "Let love be without hypocrisy" (Romans 12:9) *Agape* love cannot be faked; it is genuine, sincere, and authentic, thus – without hypocrisy.

In the latter part of the paragraph, however, Paul moves from agape love into an affectionate family love. "Be devoted to one another in brotherly love" (Romans 12:10). Here the Greek word for love *(philia)* is the same as found in Philadelphia, the city of brotherly love. Gene Getz again provides this insight: "To be devoted refers to the mutual love of parents and children and husbands and wives. It could be translated 'show loving affection' or 'love tenderly.' Paul's point is clear. Christians are to be just as devoted to each other as are the individual members in a close-knit family unit."[4] Some have suggested that Christians are *blood brothers*, and this is not a stretch to refer to ourselves in this way since "we have redemption through His blood, the forgiveness of sins" (Ephesians 1:7).

As we consider this *philia* form of love, brotherly love, God's Word is addressing not only our will, as is the case with *agape* love, but appealing to our emotions as well. Being devoted to one another in brotherly love involves affection and kindness, flowing from the genuine concern and tenderness we have for one another because of sharing life in God's family.

Paul's appeal is for Christians to display the same devotion we would see in a loyal husband or wife when the other is suffering from Alzheimer's or some other incapacitating disease. It the loving commitment shown by parents to a son or daughter with special needs, whether physical or spiritual. It is also the deep devotion we often see in sons and daughters when a parent is nearing the end of life with debilitating issues. Actions such as these are the norm in healthy families, and this is the devotion Paul is calling for in the Christian family.

As I have studied God's Word and sought to understand the meaning of this high caliber of brotherly love, I have struggled to know how to best illustrate it from Scripture. For obvious reasons, we cannot use Cain and Abel. Nor can we use Joseph and his brothers, especially during their earlier years when they sold him into slavery. We cannot use the elder brother and his younger, prodigal sibling described by Jesus in one of His most famous parables. (See Luke 15.) Two biblical examples from the Old Testament are appropriate, however, with both illustrating this deep level of loyal devotion described in our key verse for this chapter.

The first is David and Jonathan, whose enduring friendship was characterized by devotion and loyalty, displaying deep warmth and affection as well. An entire chapter could be devoted to their friendship, but I simply want to lift from Scripture a brief statement, along with a few comments. God beautifully knit the hearts of these two men together in what many see as the deepest friendship in the Bible. Their love for one another was so strong that they formed a covenant, committing themselves to one another for life. Here is a portion of it: "So Jonathan made a covenant with the house of David...and Jonathan made David vow again because of his love for him, and because he loved him as his own life" (I Samuel 20:16-17).

While their friendship was deeply tested on numerous occasions, it remained strong and continued to flourish. A careful study of their relationship reveals several selfless expressions of love, especially by Jonathan to David. When Jonathan and his father, King Saul, were killed in battle, even when David's grief was overwhelming, he spoke eloquently of how wonderful the gift of Jonathan's friendship had been, deeper than any human love David had ever known.

Years later, when David's kingdom was established and secure, the king inquired if anyone was left from the house of Jonathan. David's intent was to extend kindness to that person as an expression of the long and loyal friendship he had shared with Jonathan. The news came of a son who was still living, by the name of Mephibosheth, a man who was lame in both feet due to a serious fall he had taken as a child. David sought him out and brought him to the palace where he ate daily at the king's table, treating Mephibosheth as if he were his own son, showing him extravagant grace because of David's friendship with his father, Jonathan.

Another lovely biblical example is Ruth, a young widow from Moab, who displayed extraordinary loyalty to her Jewish mother in law, Naomi, also a grieving widow. Her classic statement has become the gold standard for the loving devotion Paul is urging in the one another command in Romans 12:10. It is spoken as Naomi is pleading with Ruth to return to her people and former way of life in Moab. Ruth's response was this: "Do not urge me to leave you or turn back from following you; for where you go, I will go, and where you lodge, I will lodge. Your people shall be my people, and your God, my God. Where you die, I will die, and there I will be buried.

Thus, may the Lord do to me if anything but death parts you and me" (Ruth 1:16-17).

Allow me to transition from these biblical examples into a more personal one from our family, a story that captures the level of loyalty described by the Apostle Paul. The main characters are two of our eight grandchildren: Brooke and Seth. Their parents are our son, Scott, and his wife and our daughter in law, Wendy. They reside in Indianapolis, our home for 24 years before moving to California in the fall of 2009.

As I write these words, Brooke is 19 and entering her sophomore year of college, and Seth 17, beginning his final year of high school. Both have birthdays this fall.

Seth is autistic, or to be more precise, he was diagnosed with ASD, Autism Spectrum Disorder. The current statistics state that 1 in 59 children in the United States are ASD, and no one knows the cause. Seth's development during the first two years of his life was as normal as any other child, showing no signs or indicators of any problems. But at some point, around the age of 2, something changed, and things began to be different. Scott and Wendy were struggling with how to deal with unexplained meltdowns in Seth's behavior, how he tended to withdraw by himself and was not as social, and why his communication skills also began to digress. Both were reading and researching what could be going on, and Linda and I were as well, seeking to find an answer to what was happening with this precious little boy we all dearly loved.

By the age of 4, Seth was enrolled in preschool classes, where he went through a battery of tests in hopes of obtaining a diagnosis. Some weeks later, after the testing was complete, the school called Scott and Wendy in for a meeting. But this time his older sister, Brooke, was 6. The teachers set up some activities for Seth in a far corner of the room, ones they knew he would enjoy. While he played alone, Scott and Wendy sat down in another part of this large room with a group of four teachers or counselors, the adults who had been observing Seth and conducting the tests. Brooke was given a seat by herself, some distance away, but close enough to hear what was being said in this meeting which lasted approximately 45 minutes. Though she was only 6, Brooke sat quietly the entire time, not part of the meeting but carefully listening. She never once interrupted or uttered a word, while Seth was occupied with his play. The difficult news communicated to Scott and Wendy was the belief that Seth was indeed ASD, autistic, an analysis consistent with his delayed communication development, and why he was behind in his social skills.

My reason for sharing this very personal story is because of what happened when the meeting was over. Brooke, only six years old, without saying a word to anyone, stood up from her chair, went over to her little brother, and gave him a long, affectionate hug! Scott, Wendy, and the four employees from the school instantly recognized that Brooke did this spontaneously. Scott's later word, when telling the story to us, was that they all had tears in their eyes. Seth's mature, six-year-old sister was expressing her love and devotion to her little brother at a time when her family had just received what she too understood to be exceedingly difficult news.

While that experience occurred several years ago, it is almost impossible to put it in writing without again having tears. I share it, however, because it captures the essence of Paul's admonition, what it means to be devoted to one another in brotherly love. Paul is urging us as brothers and sisters in Christ to show the same type of affectionate love our 6-year-old granddaughter shared with her four-year-old autistic brother. We do this because we are family, and healthy families remain devoted to one another regardless of the trial or obstacle.

Before leaving this story, I must say that to this very day Brooke continues to display an affectionate, loyal devotion to her brother. She helps him when he struggles with his homework or behavior, teaches him new things on the computer, includes him in activities with her friends, interprets for him when he is unable to communicate his needs and is always protective when someone laughs or makes fun of him. As we would say today, *she's got his back!*

In 1969, Bobby Scott and Bob Russell wrote a song that was first sung by a group called the Hollies, though several other musicians have since included it in their repertoire. While a secular song, the message touched a nerve in the hearts of many people. Here are the words: *"The road is long, with many a winding turn that leads us to who knows where. But I'm strong, strong enough to carry him, cause he ain't heavy, he's my brother. So, on we go; his welfare is my concern, no burden is he to bear, we'll get there; for I know he would not encumber me; he ain't heavy, he's my brother. If I'm laden, I'm laden with sadness, that everyone's heart is not filled with gladness, and love for one another. It's a long, long road from which there is no return; while we are on our way there, why not share, and the load doesn't weigh me down at all; cause he ain't heavy; he's my brother."* [5]

These words capture the essence of the affectionate, devoted love we are to give to one another as fellow-members in God's forever family. A major reason many are not seeing this level of commitment in their relationships is that they are simply *attending* church, but not *experiencing* it.

As we bring this chapter to a close, I want to call your attention to the last phrase in Romans 12:10, and the rest of the paragraph, leaving you with three practical applications.

First, to be devoted to one another in brotherly love includes preferring one another as being more important than ourselves. Paul's full sentence is this: "Be devoted to one another in brotherly love; give preference to one another in honor" (Romans 12:10). This devoted, brotherly love is shown when we give preference to the other person in a way that honors them without calling attention to ourselves. The Apostle Paul's words to the church in Philippi reinforce this identical truth: "Do nothing from selfishness or empty conceit, but with humility of mind regard one another as more important than yourselves; do not merely look out for your own personal interests, but also for the interests of others. Have this attitude in yourselves which was also in Christ Jesus" (Philippians 2:3-5).

A significant mark of Christian character in this tender, affectionate, brotherly love is how it thinks first about the other person. There is mutual respect between members in a healthy family; they defer to one another and find great joy when another family member is honored. Instead of thinking of our personal needs and desires, loyal family members seek what is best for the other person. In another illustration of the church, Paul again captures this truth: "When one member is honored, all the other members rejoice with it" (I Corinthians 12:26).

Second, to be devoted to one another in brotherly love includes cheerfully honoring one another with a Christlike humility. The mark of a true Christian has never been pride, nor will it ever be. Instead, it will be humility, that inner conviction of knowing that all that I am or ever will become is due only to the grace of God. Humility, however, is exceedingly elusive.

When I was a young student pastor, a wise farmer in our country church once related a story I have never forgotten. He told of another church familiar to him that decided to have a vote to determine who the members believed was the most humble person in the congregation. When the votes were all in, one elderly man received the largest number and was declared *the humblest man in the church.* As an award, they gave him a button that said, "Most humble man in the church." My farmer friend then concluded his story by explaining that the next Sunday the man wore his button, meaning the church had to immediately take it back! I do not know if that story truly happened, but if it did, I am sure it happened just that way. The point, however, is obvious; just when you think you have humility, it suddenly vanishes right before your eyes!

Another story, this one true, is of an elderly, godly teacher of God's Word. He was a member of a group to be seated on the platform at an important gathering. As he entered the room, there was suddenly the sound of applause. When he heard it, the man immediately stepped aside and began to applaud as well, thinking the ovation was for the man behind him, when it was for him. It is impossible to humbly give preference to one another in honor if we are only thinking about ourselves. Yet this is what we are called to do as an expression of our devoted, brotherly love for one another.

Third, to be devoted to one another in brotherly love includes consistently putting love in action through life's everchanging circumstances. What is so interesting about this brief paragraph (Romans 12:10-13), is how it is all linked together in the Greek language. From verse 10 through verse 13, it is all one sentence, listing ten actions describing the applicational depth of brother love.

Here is the way these verses would read: "In brotherly love, showing kindly affection; in honor to one another, giving preference; in diligence, not slothful; in spirit, fervent; in season, serving; in hope, rejoicing; in tribulation, enduring; in prayer, steadfastly continuing; to the needs of the saints, contributing; and in hospitality, pursuing." The circumstances in which we find ourselves as Christians are everchanging. These ten phrases provide us with a variety of different scenarios, along with the action of brotherly love that is needed in each instance.

May God enable us to pursue this type of love for one another, depending on our gracious Lord to make it possible.

Chapter Six Discussion Questions

1. What are some of the differences between *agape love* and *philia brotherly love*? What are the similarities? How are both meant to be part of relational Christianity?
2. How can those who came from dysfunctional homes, or grew up without a real home, come to experience the church as a healthy family? What is needed for this to happen? Do you have an example of someone who found the church to be the family they never knew?
3. What does the author say about family not being a metaphor but an actual description of those who know God as their Father?
4. What needs to happen for Christians to view each Sunday gathering as a *mini family reunion*? What truths do we need to embrace to see the church in this way?
5. In addition to the loyal friendship between David and Jonathan, and that of Ruth and Naomi, can you think of other biblical examples or historical examples of brotherly love? To what extent have you found friendships of this depth in the church?

Chapter Seven
Be Hospitable to One Another

"Be hospitable to one another without complaint."

I Peter 4:9

In his enlightening and stimulating book, *The Hospitality Commands*, Alexander Strauch tells of an elderly woman in his church, a friend who at an earlier time in life, attended a suburban church. Each Sunday after the morning service, she would eat alone in a restaurant and then spend Sunday afternoon in a park, or the library, so she could attend the evening service. She did this for four years. While she loved many things about the church to keep her coming that long, what left her with somewhat sour memories was the fact that in four years, not one person had invited her into their home for a meal, or to rest. It was not until this lady announced that she was leaving, that one elderly woman in the church invited her for lunch on her final Sunday.[1]

When I read that story, I wondered how many lonely people have been in the churches where we have served who are like this lady. How many of the people we greet on Sunday mornings would benefit if we would value them enough to invite them into our homes, demonstrating Christian hospitality?

A few years ago, in our church in Porterville, we had a charming young lady from Idaho join us for worship one Sunday. We learned she was in the area for several months, working with horses at a ranch in the foothills of the Sierras. Because she had such a winsome personality and enthusiasm about Christ, several of us found it easy to invite her into our homes. As a result, we built a lasting relationship, one that has continued, long after her stay among us was over. The reality, however, is that not everyone who comes into our churches, whether young, old, or in between, is as engaging and easy to recognize, yet all would benefit from loving hospitality.

After graduating from seminary in 1968, Linda and I, along with our amiable 3-year-old, Cheryl, bid farewell to my home state of Kentucky for Tyler, Texas to join the ministry of a healthy church God would use for the next 17 years to shape our lives, our family, and our ministry. One of the couples that made a lasting impression on us, and are still friends today, was David and Myrlene Florey. It was not until some years later when we learned that they prepared extra food each Sunday for the precise purpose of spontaneously inviting someone home after church. During our years of ministry at Grace Community in Tyler, we heard numerous families state that their first meaningful contact with the church was around Dave and Myrlene's dining room table. We also benefited from the Florey family's ministry as they invited us to join them for our first Thanksgiving in Texas, aware that we were without relatives in the area and a long way from home.

Rosaria Butterfield was an outspoken unbeliever before coming to Christ through an invitation to dinner in a modest home from a pastor and his wife who lived out the gospel simply and authentically. Now a pastor's wife herself, she and her husband use their home as a base to share the Gospel. Demonstrating radical and what most would consider sacrificial hospitality, Rosaria has extra food on the stove *daily* to serve to anyone the Lord chooses to bring into their lives. In her book, *The Gospel Comes with a House Key*,[2] she eloquently shares her passion, communicating that we as believers are not to view our homes as our own, but as God's tool for the furtherance of His kingdom.

While Linda and I have progressively sought to embrace hospitality, it has been a learning process. As is always the case when God brings a lasting change in our lives, His Word was a key part in our training. In my study of the church in Acts, for example, I discovered that hospitality was a distinctive hallmark; it was the way the first-century church put Christ's love in action. The result was that Christ's followers multiplied exponentially across the Roman Empire, even though church buildings did not begin to be constructed until the 3rd century. While the phenomenal growth can be attributed to several factors, one of the most significant was hospitality, as enthusiastic new believers opened their hearts and homes to one another. On several occasions, we see in the New Testament the phrase "the church that meets in their house" (Romans 16:5; Colossians 4:15; Philemon 1:2, etc.). The same pattern is followed today in countries where construction of church buildings is simply not possible; the Body of Christ grows through the establishment of house churches, meaning loving hospitality is practiced by many families.

In addition to the historical account in Acts, the New Testament epistles to the various churches contain several directives about hospitality. From these passages, I want to lift six principles that have been helpful to me in embracing this valuable one another truth.

First, hospitality is an expression of brotherly love. Again, Alexander Strauch observes, "The biblical injunctions to practice hospitality are nearly always found in the context of brotherly love."[3] While the New Testament writers employ several metaphors in describing the church (Flock, Bride, Body, Temple, Kingdom, Vineyard, Building), to refer to the church as a family, however, is not a metaphor; it is literally who we are. God is our Father and we are His children by grace alone through faith alone in Christ alone, meaning that all Christians are brothers and sisters in Christ. The hospitality we are called to show is to our family.

The prophet, Malachi, once asked, "Have we not all one Father? Has not God created us? (Malachi 2:10) In his letter to the church at Ephesus, the Apostle Paul, stating the identical truth positively, answered Malachi's question, "There is one God and Father of all who is over all and through all and in all" (Ephesians 4:6). The first-century Christians referred to one another as brother and sister because they recognized this as their identity. The terms *brother and sister* are found in the New Testament more than 250 times. When we examine the context of the hospitality admonitions, each one is linked in some way to this profound family love.

One of the most attractive features of the first-century church is how their hospitality transcended all national, racial, and social boundaries. Their perspective was, "There is neither Jew nor Greek, there is neither slave nor free man, there is neither male nor female; for you are all one in Christ Jesus" (Galatians 3:28). The more we embrace our biblical identity as God's children, the more comfortable we become in showing hospitality.

While Christian hospitality was deeply valued and practiced by the early Christians, many Christians in America today fail to embrace its importance, perhaps due to our affluence. In other parts of the world, however, especially in third world nations, it continues to be lived out. Dr. Samuel Kamalasen, a missionary statesman from India, once came to our church in Texas for a mission's conference. In one of his sermons, he made a statement I have never forgotten: *The poor of this world are never lacking in hospitality.* I have experienced this in my trips to Haiti, and the rural areas of the Dominican Republic. My wife, Linda, and I have also been the recipients of it during numerous visits in several parts of Mexico, as well as among the primitive tribal peoples in Irian Jaya, now Papua, Indonesia. Our experience is that Christians living in challenging circumstances always seek to give all who come among them their absolute best, whether the best seat, the best bed, the best piece of meat, or the best food from their garden, whatever it may be.

Second, hospitality is a virtue we are commanded to pursue. We see this in the application section of Paul's epistle to the church in Rome. Paul makes it clear that pursuing healthy relationships is one of the primary marks of one who has been transformed by the Gospel of grace. "Be devoted to one another in brotherly love; give preference to one another in honor, contributing to the needs of the saints, practicing hospitality" (Romans 12:10, 13).

Here again, hospitality is mentioned in the context of faithful family love. While the NASB translates the phrase, *practicing hospitality,* the ESV renders it more literally, "Seek to show hospitality" (Romans 12:13 ESV[4]). The idea is *to strive for or pursue,* conveying that we are to be deliberate and purposeful in it.

My wife, Linda, and I have sought to be hospitable from the early years of our marriage. A significant factor was that she grew up in a loving, hospitable, missionary family in Medellin, Colombia, where guests were welcomed regularly into their home. My parents in Appalachia were also hospitable to my friends, and even more so after coming to Christ. In the first five years of our marriage when I was serving as a student pastor, the families in our small country churches consistently modeled hospitality to us, having us into their homes for lunch and dinner every Sunday, and gladly opening their homes anytime we needed to spend the night. We are blessed with many exemplary mentors in this vital ministry.

While we were pursuing hospitality from the beginning there were times when we did not get it right. In the early 1970s, through the generosity of a family in the church, we were able to rent a lovely home in Tyler, Texas, for a price we could afford with our budget. We can recall several people we hosted during that time, some for extended periods. One was a young, single farmer from Japan. He was not a believer but had been exposed to the Gospel through an English class led by Dick and Judy Amos (Linda's sister), career missionaries in Japan. This young man was coming to tour America, riding the Greyhound bus cross country, and would be coming through Tyler at some point, and would contact us. Judy and Dick, Linda's sister, and her husband asked if we would host him for a few days to give him a taste of what an American home was like. They informed us that while he did not know English very well, he was bold in seeking to communicate.

We gladly agreed but did not hear anything from him until late one Saturday afternoon, New Year's Eve, when he called from the bus station in Tyler. I drove down to pick him up while Linda tidied up the house for our Japanese guest. We first gave him something to eat, arranged for him to meet with a group of singles from our church, and waited up until he returned. We did our best to communicate that he should *make himself at home.* We had what we felt was a nice room for guests with matching day beds, covered with attractive material such as would be on a couch. Linda gave our Japanese guest a pillow, a towel, and washcloth, showed him the bathroom, and then said good night. A couple of days passed, and things seemed to be progressing well, though we were frequently using his Japanese/English dictionary. On the third evening, before going to bed, he again pulled out his dictionary and asked, "May I have a..." and then he pointed to the word, "blanket?" We could not understand why he needed a blanket since the temperature of our home was comfortable. But when we walked with him into his room, the problem we never suspected suddenly became clear; we pulled back the cover of the day bed to reveal the sheets and blankets that were already on the bed. He did not know to pull the cover of the day bed back, and we did not think to tell him. We were embarrassed, and so was he. This young, wealthy Japanese farmer was sleeping on top of the day bed, using his coat for a *blanket.* Eventually, we all had a good laugh about it, and we also learned a needed lesson in hospitality – never assume anything, especially with a guest from a different culture.

Third, hospitality is to be practiced with a cheerful attitude. When the Apostle Peter was addressing believers who were undergoing deep trials because of their faith, he wrote, "Above all, keep fervent in your love for one another, because love covers a multitude of sins. Be hospitable to one another without complaint" (I Peter 4:8-9). Here again, the hospitality command accompanies an admonition to love. Peter's command is stated negatively (without complaint) while I have stated the same truth positively - with a cheerful attitude.

In our first years in Porterville, we had some young girls in our neighborhood who dearly loved Linda. They enjoyed coming to our home, and a few of them soon began attending Wednesday night AWANA classes with us at church. One of them, Aspen, who was 11 years old at the time, gave me a Charlie Brown (Peanuts) book to read on happiness. One of the pages stated, "Happiness is seeing the faces of good friends at your front door." [5] I like that! When Aspen and her friend, Marina, would come to our door in the weeks following, in greeting them I would always say, "Happiness is seeing the faces of good friends at your front door!" Charlie Brown's words were a good reminder to be hospitable to one another cheerfully and without complaint.

Fourth, hospitality brings unexpected benefits. In the book of Hebrews, we read this captivating admonition, "Keep on loving one another as brothers and sisters. Do not neglect to show hospitality to strangers, for by this some have entertained angels without knowing it" (Hebrews 13:1-2).

The word about entertaining angels without knowing it certainly makes hospitality more intriguing. The application point we can safely make from the text is that even if we do not receive a visit from angels, hospitality brings surprising benefits.

One biblical example is of Cleopas and his friend the afternoon of Christ's resurrection. They were traveling from

Jerusalem to their home in Emmaus, a journey of approximately seven miles. While they were walking and having an animated discussion about the events of the previous days, which culminated in the crucifixion of Jesus, Jesus Himself suddenly drew near and began to walk along with them. The text records, however, that their eyes were prevented from recognizing Him. (Read Luke 24:13-35 for the full account.) That afternoon walk to Emmaus was life-changing for Cleopas and his friend, as has the reading of their experience been for believers for more than 2,000 years. Interestingly, the high moment when they recognized that the wise and gracious stranger was Jesus, occurred through an expression of hospitality. "And they approached the village where they were going, and He acted as though He were going farther. But they urged Him, saying, 'Stay with us, for it is getting toward evening'" (Luke 24:28-29). Jesus gladly accepted their kind invitation. Luke continues: "When He reclined at the table with them, He took the bread and blessed it, and breaking it began giving it to them. Then their eyes were opened, and they recognized Him; and He vanished from their sight" (Luke 24:30-31). As they reflected on how He, as their guest, unexpectedly became their Host, gratefully breaking and sharing bread, their words were these: "Were not our hearts burning within us while He was speaking to us on the road, and while He was explaining the Scriptures to us" (Luke 24:32).

As we extend hospitality, whether to friends or strangers, while we may not entertain angels, or Jesus Himself, such as Cleophas and his friend in their Emmaus home, God will certainly surprise us with delightful benefits. One of the most heartening serendipities is seeing how additional one another's spontaneously begin to occur in an atmosphere of genuine hospitality. This is certainly how it has been with groups in our home.

Two years before our visit by the Japanese farmer, we had another man from Japan, a gracious, respected leader in the church in Japan, who came to our church in Texas for six months. His purpose was to learn about discipleship from our ministry and to audit classes in a nearby seminary. Six of our families would open our homes, making it possible for him to stay for one month with each family. Linda and I were one of those families, and what a delight it was.

His name was Etsuo Matsumura, but the Japanese referred to him as Matsumura Sensei, a title of utmost respect given to esteemed teachers. When he first arrived, we introduced him on a Sunday morning to our people and asked him to greet our church. He had worked on his introductory speech, and it was one none of us will ever forget. He began by saying quite deliberately, *"Since I have been in America, I have seen many things which say, 'Made in Japan.' I was also made in Japan, made by God in Japan."* With that initial greeting, he instantly won the hearts of our people. Matsumura Sensei had a Christlike attitude and spirit, making him a wonderful blessing in our home. The other families who opened their homes received immeasurable blessings as well.

Some years later, we hosted his son, Kyoto, who lived with us for an extended period as he attended the Christian school established by our church. Our children will always remember Kyoto practicing his karate chops and kicks all through our home. When I made a ministry trip to Japan in 1984, and Linda and our daughter, Christy, the following year, the Matsumura family gave us a royal welcome. Hospitality has reciprocal benefits, and Linda and I could give story after story of how God has blessed and enriched our entire family through those we invited into our homes and lives.

Fifth, hospitality is to be practiced as if we were hosting our Lord. While this may appear to be an impossible goal to attain, to the degree that we can view hospitality in this light, our ministry to others will be greatly enhanced. Interestingly, this perspective comes from the instruction of Jesus Himself. A few years ago, the

Holy Spirit used Jesus' words to elevate my wife, Linda's, way of looking at the arrival of guests.

Wherever we have lived, we have asked God to use us in our neighborhood in whatever way He desired; this was our prayer when we moved to Porterville in the fall of 2009. As I mentioned earlier, after settling into our neighborhood, we became acquainted with several young girls belonging to the families who lived near us. They soon grew to love Linda like a grandmother, and she planned tea parties for them, baked cookies, and other memorable activities. During those years I would jokingly comment that the girls would often come to the door and ask, *"Can Linda come out and play?"*

While all this was wonderful, it was not always easy for Linda to drop what she was doing to warmly welcome the girls when they came by. Sometimes she would ask them to come back in a couple of hours or make some alternate plan because of her other responsibilities. Her perspective changed one day when the words of Jesus came to her mind, "Whoever welcomes one such child in My name welcomes Me" (Matthew 18:5). From that point on, Linda explained that when the girls came to our door, she sought to visualize Jesus standing there with them! Jesus, in His famous parable in Matthew 25, convincingly makes this point, "I was hungry, and you gave Me something to eat; I was thirsty, and you gave Me something to drink; I was a stranger, and you invited Me in... to the extent that you did it to one of these brothers of Mine, even the least of them, you did it to Me" (Matthew 25:35, 40). There is strong biblical support to indicate that each loving act we do as believers should be done with this perspective, "Whatever you do, do your work heartily, as for the Lord rather than for men" (Colossians 3:23).

Whether you are aware of it or not, God is constantly at work to renew your mind, enabling you to think biblically with a Christian mindset. How many of us need to have our minds and perspectives renewed concerning hospitality? I continue to stand in need, and God has been at work renewing my mind as I write this chapter.

Sixth, hospitality is one of the qualifications for elders in the church. This is not surprising when we understand that the church met in homes during the first two centuries, and it continues to be the pattern in many parts of the world. At the heart of being an elder is the ministry of shepherding, and a vital part of this is being able to lovingly welcome people into one's home.

One of my favorite Biblical examples of a hospitable elder is found in the little postcard epistle of Philemon. Paul wrote the letter from prison in Rome on behalf of Philemon's runaway slave, Onesimus, who came to faith in Christ while in the same prison as the Apostle Paul. Paul's letter is an appeal to his friend, urging him to welcome Onesimus back, not merely as a slave, but as a new brother in Christ. It appears that Philemon was one of the pastor/elders in Colossae, with the church meeting in his home, and his wife and son sharing in this ministry. This is where the example of hospitality surfaces. Paul commends Philemon for his love for all the saints and then writes, "I have come to have much joy and comfort in your love because *the hearts of the saints have been refreshed through you, brother*" (Philemon 7; italics mine).

Hospitality, when carried out with a Christlike attitude, never fails to bring spiritual refreshment to those who receive it, along with a great joy to those demonstrating it. This is likely why Alexander Strauch refers to hospitality as *the crown jewel in Christian life and service*[6]. Sadly, it is a jewel that is often missing, even in churches where the Bible is faithfully taught.

Early in our journey of seeking to be hospitable, we discovered Karen Main's enlightening book, *Open Heart, Open Home*. Writing as the wife of a pastor, one of her most helpful insights for us was her enlightening distinction between entertaining and hospitality. She writes: "Entertaining says, 'I want to impress people with my beautiful home, my clever decorating, and my gourmet cooking'. Hospitality, however, seeks to minister. It says, 'This home is not mine. It is truly a gift from my Master. I am His servant, and want to use it as He desires.' Hospitality does not try to impress, but to serve."[8]

In my 50 plus years as a pastor, Linda and I recognize that our home has unquestionably been one of our most fruitful places of ministry. Within the broad range of pastoral responsibilities, hospitality may be viewed by some as relatively small and insignificant, but we have witnessed the lasting impact on those we have hosted, and the extraordinary blessing it has brought to our entire family.

My prayer is that God has used this chapter to give you a more open heart toward people, leading to an open home where others can be spiritually refreshed.

Chapter Seven Discussion Questions

1. Describe the most loving expression of hospitality you have received, and what made it so positive and memorable.
2. There is an obvious link between greeting and being hospitable to the guests who come among us. How could an otherwise healthy church fail to be hospitable to the lady the author describes in the opening paragraph of this chapter? How can prevent this from happening in our church?
3. What attitude changes are needed for Christians to *pursue hospitality and* make the home God has entrusted to them a base for ministry?
4. The author describes how hospitality brings serendipitous blessings, one of them being that additional *one another's* begin to occur. Why do you think this is so? Is this something you have observed?
5. Read again Matthew 25:35, 40 and discuss how Jesus' words are meant to shape our view of hospitality.
6. According to Karen Mains, what is the difference between entertaining and hospitality? While there is nothing wrong with wanting to welcome guests with excellence, how can we make sure we are truly focusing on their needs?
7. What is the biggest lesson you have learned about hospitality?

Chapter Eight
"Let Us Not Judge One Another."

"Therefore let us not judge one another anymore."

Romans 14:13

At some point in our lives, each one of us has likely passed judgment on someone without having all the facts. Sometimes the only outcome is an embarrassment, while at other times people are deeply hurt, and the name of Christ is put to shame.

A year or so after we moved to California, I came face to face with my fleshly tendency to rush to premature judgments. It happened soon after I joined a gym in the area to get more exercise. In addition to the physical benefits, I also met some interesting people, one being a man I became acquainted with soon after I joined. In our initial conversation, we learned a few basic facts about each other; we were similar in age, both married, and had children and grandchildren. In our exchange, we also mentioned that neither of our wives was coming to the gym.

A few days later, I noticed my new friend having a jovial conversation with a woman at the gym, also around our age. The first time I did not think much about it since I also seek to be friendly with everyone I meet. But as the days went by, I noticed how this man kept seeking out the same lady, as if being pulled toward her by a magnet. There was an obvious warmth between them; nothing physical, but an attraction.

My private thought was that his affection was more than I would feel comfortable sharing with another woman. Though I said nothing to anyone, in my judgment I questioned whether his actions were appropriate. While I reflected on the fact that we were *old men in our 70s*, with our bodies decaying, becoming broken down, and decrepit, my belief was that, whatever our age, we still need to be careful about how we relate to members of the opposite sex. In my judgment, my new friend was crossing the line. But, as I said, all this was in my thoughts; I had said nothing about it to anyone.

A few days later, as I came up the stairs, there they were again, talking warmly, laughing with each other, and having a great time. When he saw me, he greeted me and said, *"By the way, Tom, have you met my sister?"* I don't know if he could see the look of shock and shame on my face, or the rebuke I felt in my heart upon learning that his relationship with this woman was not inappropriate at all, as I had judged it to be. SHE WAS HIS SISTER! That possibility never once crossed my mind; I was too busy judging my friend without having all the facts! I feel certain you have done the same thing.

Having been a pastor for more than five decades, there have been occasions when someone made a casual comment to me about another person in the church, not intending to be judgmental, but words revealing that this person had formed an opinion about a brother or sister in Christ, such as I did with my friend at the gym, one based on very limited information. Because pastors generally know parishioners a little better than others in the church, there have been times when I have thought - *If you truly understood their situation, and where they are coming from, your opinion would be far different from the one you just expressed.* At times, when I felt it was appropriate and I was not betraying someone's confidence, I have spoken gentle words to help the person understand there was more to that person's story than what they had expressed in their comment. But isn't this always how it is? Our knowledge of each other's lives and circumstances is extremely limited. This being so, how could we pass judgment on one another? Yet we do it to our detriment, our shame, our embarrassment, and often we deeply hurt a brother or sister in Christ in the process.

For this reason, the *one another* which is our focus in this chapter is vitally important to the relational health of the church: "Let us not judge one another anymore" (Romans 14:13). Paul adding the word *anymore* to his command implies that judging was going on and needed to be stopped.

As we examine God's Word about this crucial command, we will look at two primary passages: Romans 14 and I Corinthians 4. While both deal with judging, they approach it from opposite perspectives. Paul's instruction in Romans 14 is directed toward Christians who were making judgments about one another, whereas his words in I Corinthians 4 are written from the perspective of the one being judged or evaluated.

We turn first to the matter of judging others, which in Rome had its origin in the extremely diverse backgrounds of those in the church. The Jewish believers, for example, had been saved out of a strict, legalistic background that was difficult for them to fully forsake. In contrast, the Gentile believers had nothing in their pagan background about special diets they were to follow or holy days they were required to observe but were being pressured by some of the Jews to adhere to these practices.

As Paul writes to this diverse group, he makes it clear that the judgments they were making about one another were not about biblical absolutes; they were over issues each person had to work out in his own heart before the Lord, even as Paul summarizes: "Each person must be fully convinced in his own mind" (Romans 14:5). The problems had arisen because certain ones were failing to give others freedom in these matters. Instead, they were judging one another by their own beliefs and convictions instead of rejoicing in the common faith they had come to share in Christ. This is often a reason we too are quick to judge one another; we fail to take into consideration that the brother or sister with whom we are struggling is coming from an entirely different background, with a vastly different way of thinking. We need to see that what matters most is knowing Christ, keeping Him preeminent, maintaining our unity, and loving one another.

Pauls' instruction, while written to correct problems which had surfaced in the church at Rome, also communicates timeless truths to help us overcome our fleshly tendency to judge one another. At least three principles emerge from Paul's words.

First, we do not have adequate knowledge or proper authority to accurately judge others. This was certainly the case with my friend at the gym (who is now part of our church family). My judgment was based on extremely limited information, along with the truth that it was not my position to judge him.

As Paul addressed the problem, his challenge was not only to younger believers but to the more mature as well. "Now accept the one who is weak in faith, but not for the purpose of passing judgment on his opinions...who are you to judge the servant of another? To his own master he stands or falls; and he will stand, for the Lord is the one who is able to make him stand" (Romans 14:1,3-4). Instead of hastily passing judgment on a brother or sister who was relatively new to the Christian faith, the more mature believers were to lovingly accept them for where they were in their Christian growth. The same principle applied to the new believers who were judging those older in the faith, whose ideas they did not yet understand. Paul makes it clear that if we do judge, we are overstepping our bounds; we have no authority to judge someone who is the servant of another.

Second, each person who is a member of God's family has already been accepted by Him. In Paul's instruction regarding the cultural issues in the church at Rome, he writes, "The one who eats is not to regard with contempt the one who does not eat, and the one who does not eat is not to judge the one who eats, for God has accepted him" (Romans 14:3). Even though there were significant differences, the bottom line was that God had accepted each one, and that was all that mattered. Contempt for one of God's children by another who also claims to be a Christian is an attitude that has no place in the church. This is the point we saw in an earlier chapter: "Accept one another, even as Christ has accepted us to the glory of God" (Romans 15:7). How can we as fellow believers and brothers and sisters in God's family, reject and treat with contempt someone whom God has fully accepted through His Son?

An instructive example of overcoming this tendency to judge comes from the life of Simon Peter, as God worked to remove his prejudice toward the Gentiles. Though it required a supernatural vision from heaven, once Peter saw the truth, he responded wholeheartedly, going without hesitation into the home of Cornelius, an Italian centurion, to share the transforming message of the gospel. These are his words: "You yourselves know how unlawful it is for a man who is a Jew to associate with a foreigner or to visit with him, yet God has shown me that I should not consider any man unholy or unclean. This is why I came to you without raising objections" (Acts 10:28-29). Peter's words challenge me to search my heart to make sure I have responded to God's plan to bring me to the same conclusion; *I will not consider any man unholy or unclean.* When the Holy Spirit works in our hearts to this extent, our inclination to judge is greatly reduced, if not taken away altogether.

A third related point is this: *all true believers are servants of the Lord Jesus Christ, and He enables each one to stand regardless of judgments others make against them.* Whether one is a weak Christian or a strong mature believer, God is the common Master of all His servants, and no one is to interfere with that relationship. Paul convincingly makes his point with these words, "Who are you to judge the servant of another? To his own master he stands or falls; and he will stand, for God is able to make Him stand" (Romans 14:4).

Don't you love those words? If you are a true Christian who has responded to God's gracious call, you will be able to keep on standing, not because of your strength and determination, but because Almighty God will make sure you stand. Salvation is from the Lord from first to last; to Him be all the glory! "Being confident of this very thing, that He who began a good work in you will continue to perfect it to the day of Jesus Christ" (Philippians 1:6). "Even if we are faithless (unfaithful), He remains faithful, for He cannot deny Himself" (II Timothy 2:13).

We turn now to I Corinthians 4 to examine judging from the other side, that of the person being judged. Though Paul was an apostle, he was constantly in the position of being judged and evaluated by others.

To understand Paul's words, it is important to know that the church in Corinth was inundated by division and disunity. The church had separated into different groups with some declaring their allegiance to Peter, others to Apollos, and still others to Paul. Another faction claimed to follow Christ but did so with an arrogant attitude of contempt toward those in the other groups.

Paul wrote several corrective words to the church, but a significant part of his answer was to clarify who he and the other men in leadership were before the Lord: "Let a man regard us in this manner, as servants of Christ and stewards of the mysteries of God" (I Corinthians 4:1). If this fundamental truth could be embraced, the question would no longer be if Apollos was a better preacher than Paul or Peter, or if Peter should have their allegiance because of his long history with the church, or if Paul should be followed because he was the one who brought them the Gospel. If the church could understand that these men were first and foremost servants of Christ, and stewards who were accountable to their common Lord, the divisions could be dissolved, and the church return to health.

Earlier in his letter, Paul made essentially the same point, only with different words: "What then is Apollos? And what is Paul? Servants through whom you believed, even as the Lord gave opportunity to each one. I planted, Apollos watered, but God was causing the growth. So then neither the one who plants nor the one who waters is anything, but God who causes the growth" (I Corinthians 3:5-7).

The blunt reality, however, for all who are leaders in the church, is that you are going be evaluated, criticized, and judged. This is one reason why James gave the warning he did: "Let not many of you become teachers, my brothers, knowing we incur a stricter judgment" (James 3:1). Those who listen to you speak and observe your life are going to make judgments on how well you are doing your job, how you relate to people, along with how things are in your marriage, family, and personal life. This being the case, how are you going to respond when you are *judged* by others?

What is so helpful about this passage is the way Paul opens his heart to reveal how he responded to the judgments and opinions of others.

First, *do not be overly concerned when others pass judgment on you.* Paul begins with these words: "To me, it is a very small thing that I should be examined by you, or by any human court" (I Corinthians 4:3). I will be the first to confess that this is a difficult position to take. When other people examine or make judgments about me, it can be painful. When I am criticized, it can easily become a time of stress. Not one of us enjoys being judged. The inclination of most is to avoid times when we are to be evaluated like the plague! Part of this is our insecurity, or because we are living to please others; our desire is for others to respect and think highly of us. Perhaps the most significant factor is that we have forgotten that our foremost calling is to live our lives to an audience of One, that One being the Lord Jesus Christ! Because Paul's highest goal was to please Christ, being examined or judged by others was a small thing to him.

Second, *do not be overly confident in your judgment of yourself.* Paul continues: "In fact, I don't even examine myself. I am conscious of nothing against myself, but this does not mean that I am acquitted" (I Corinthians 4:3-4). Each one of us will go through periods of self-evaluation, but our judgment is not the ultimate verdict that acquits us. As Christians we are aware that God's Word teaches us to search and examine our hearts each time we participate in communion – the Lord's Table. In his second letter to the church in Corinth, the Apostle Paul also admonished those in the church: "Test yourselves to see if you are in the faith; examine yourselves! Or do you not recognize this about yourselves that Jesus Christ is in you - unless indeed you fail the test" (II Corinthians 13:5). To see if we are in the faith is the most important self-examination of all, and we can only do this when we have an awareness of how God's Word defines one who is a genuine believer.

Third, *give your utmost attention to the judgment you will receive from the Lord.* Paul continues, "But the one who examines me is the Lord" (I Corinthians 4:4). Paul understood that it was the Lord's judgment alone that was not only accurate but final. Though his critics could level their accusations against him; and while he could search his own heart to see if there was within him any evil way, neither of those evaluations mattered when compared to what the Lord would ultimately say to him.

In Paul's second letter to the church in Corinth, he returns to this truth: "We have as our ambition, whether at home or absent, to be pleasing to Him. For we must all appear before the judgment seat of Christ so that each one may be recompensed for his deeds in the body, according to what he has done, whether good or bad (II Corinthians 5:9-10).

The MacArthur Study Bible has this helpful explanation of how the judgment of Christians differs from that of unbelievers: "This judgment does not include sins, since their judgment took place on the cross (Ephesians 1:7). Paul was referring to those activities that believers do during their lifetime, which related to eternal reward and praise from God. What Christians do in their temporal bodies will, in His eyes, have an impact for eternity."[1] The Bible describes this event in terms of how we build on the sure and only foundation of Christ: "But each man must be careful how he builds upon it. For no man can lay a foundation other than the one which is laid, which is Jesus Christ" (I Corinthians 3:10-11). He goes on to speak of flawed building materials which will be consumed in the fire, but also of the appropriate building materials which will stand the test of the judgment seat of Christ.

A helpful explanation of the phrase "whether good or bad" (the final phrase in II Corinthians 5:10) is also found in the MacArthur Study Bible: "These Greek terms (good or bad) do not refer to moral good or moral evil. Matters of sin have been completely dealt with by the death of the Savior. Rather, Paul was comparing worthwhile, eternally valuable activities with useless ones. His point was not that believers should never enjoy certain wholesome, earthly things; but that they should glorify God in them, and spend most of their energy and time with what has eternal value."[2] This being said, even though Christ has taken our sin upon Himself and clothed us with His righteousness, it is nevertheless, a sobering thought to know that we will be evaluated as to how we have built our lives on Him as our sure foundation.

Fourth: *the judgments of others are always premature; our Lord's judgment is final.* In the first four verses of the chapter, Paul was writing of his own experience, whereas in verse 5 he began to make application for the church: "Therefore, do not go on passing judgment before the time, but wait until the Lord comes" (I Corinthians 4:5). Whatever judgments made of us by others are never final; it is when the Lord evaluates our lives and ministries that the judgment will be absolute. Anything before that is premature and incomplete.

Fifth, *the judgments of others have fluctuating standards; our Lord's judgment is based on His word.* The people in the immature, divided church in Corinth were making judgments based on personal preferences and prejudices, even as we often do when we *judge* others. Their judgments were also based on comparisons, a practice we are strongly warned against in Scripture: "We are not so bold to class or compare ourselves with some who commend themselves; but when they measure themselves by themselves and compare themselves among themselves, they are without understanding" (II Corinthians 10:12). The only true and final standard of judgment is God's Word. But even then, God's evaluation will be based on our individual calling and gifts. Like Paul, Peter, and Apollos, we are *servants of Christ and stewards of the mysteries of God.* Each one of us will be accountable in the same way; have we been faithful servants of Christ and faithful stewards of everything He entrusted to us.

Sixth, *the judgments of others evaluate actions; our Lord's judgment is based on motives as well.* Take a close look at Paul's further words of application: "Wait until the Lord comes, who will both bring to light the things hidden in darkness and disclose the *motives* of men's hearts, and then each man's praise will come to himself from God" (I Corinthians 4:5; italics mine).

What a day this will be! Not only is the Lord alone able to see everything that takes place in the darkness; He is also the only one who can reveal the secret motives in our hearts. Consequently, as Paul writes in the key verse of this chapter, "Let us not judge one another anymore" (Romans 14:13). Though we may think we know our motives, our judgments can be flawed, for we often have mixed motives; we desire to glorify God, while at the same time calling attention to ourselves.

When we truly know who God is and that our accountability is to Him as our final Judge, these truths can set us free from our fleshly tendency to rush to judgment about others without knowing the facts.

Chapter Eight Discussion Questions

1. Describe a time when you passed judgment about someone without knowing all the facts. What was the outcome? Was someone hurt or was there only embarrassment?
2. What are some of the factors that contribute to us being judgmental toward others? What biblical truths are highlighted in this chapter to help us avoid and overcome judgmental attitudes?
3. Why was the Apostle Paul able to say that it was a small thing to be examined by others, or even when he examined himself? How do these truths apply to us?
4. How does the Lord's judgment of believers differ from the judgment of unbelievers? What are the criteria for the judgment of believers? What about the judgment of unbelievers?
5. What part do motives play in making it difficult if not impossible to judge others, and even judge ourselves?
6. How should the knowledge that we will be judged based on how we have built on Christ as our only foundation impact how we live?
7. What is one application related to judging you will seek to make from this chapter?

Chapter Nine
"Forgive One Another."

"Be kind to one another, tender-hearted, forgiving each other, just as God in Christ has forgiven you."

Ephesians 4:32

"Bearing with one another, and forgiving each other, whoever has a complaint against anyone; just as the Lord forgave you, so also should you."

Colossians 3:13

When I preach or teach on forgiveness, I often use a story of a married couple Jay Adams tells about in his book, *Christian Living in the Home,* because it provides an excellent launching point into this all-important topic. "Sue and Wilbur came for counseling. She sat there with arms defiantly folded, he nervously shifting from side to side. You could see before either said a word what it was going to be like. She opened the conversation from her side of the desk with these words: 'I am here because my physician sent me. He said there is nothing physically wrong with me. He said I'm getting an ulcer but not from any physical cause.' All the while, her husband sat there cowering. Sue reached down into what looked like a shopping bag (it was her purse), and pulled out a manuscript that was at least one inch thick, on 8 ½ x 11 size paper, single-spaced, typewritten on both sides. She slapped it down on the counselor's desk and said, 'That's why I'm getting an ulcer.' He said, 'Is that a fact?' and looked at it. He could not have read it in a month, even if he cared to. But as he spot-checked through it, flipping along, he saw immediately what it was. It turned out to be a thirteen-year record of wrongs her husband had done to her. They were all listed and cataloged. Now, what would you have said to her? The counselor looked at Sue and said, 'It's been a long time since I met anyone as resentful as you.' She was a little taken back, and Wilbur sat up a little straighter. The counselor continued, 'This is not only a record of what your husband has done to you (incidentally, subsequent sessions showed that it was a very accurate record), it is also a record of what you have done about it. This is a record of your sin against him, your sin against God, and your sin against your own body. This is a record you cannot deny, for you put it down in black and white. This record of bitterness shows that your attitude has been the opposite of I Corinthians 13, where Scripture says that love never keeps a record of wrongs suffered.'"[1]

Jay Adams went on to point out how difficult it would be to deal with the problems in Sue and Wilbur's marriage until she faced her sin of failing to forgive. Wilbur certainly had numerous areas in his life that needed to change, but Sue's lack of forgiveness, which had turned into resentment and deep root of bitterness, had to be honestly faced before any significant progress could be made.

Interestingly, the question raised in the story of Sue and Wilbur is identical to the one Simon Peter asked Jesus: "Lord, how often shall my brother sin against me, and I forgive him? Seven times?" (Matthew 18:21) To fully appreciate Peter's question it is helpful to understand that the Jewish rabbis in Jesus' day had a teaching that a man must forgive his brother three times.[2] They based this on their flawed belief that God's forgiveness only extended to three offenses, and then He would punish the offender on the fourth offense. Peter appears to have been taking the popular teaching of the day, multiplying it by two, and then adding one more for good measure.

The response Jesus gave was shocking to Peter and unforgettable to all who heard it; it continues to astonish us even today. "Jesus said to him, 'I do not say unto you seven times, but up to seventy times seven" (Matthew 18:22). Multiply this out and it comes to 490; according to Jesus, we are to forgive one another not three times, or even seven times, but 70 x 7 = 490 times! When we look more carefully at what Jesus was saying, we discover that this was His way of declaring that forgiveness is to be limitless.

To further illuminate His point, Jesus proceeded to tell the story of a king who decided to settle accounts with his servants, telling of one who owed the king the incredible sum of 10 thousand talents. With the talent being the largest denomination of money at the time, 10 thousand talents represented an incomprehensible debt, an infinite amount.[3] Jesus was making the point that a person's debt to God is so great that it could never, under any circumstances, be paid back any more than a servant working for a few cents a day could ever save up enough money to repay a debt of 10 thousand talents.

But Jesus, the master storyteller, was not finished. He went on to describe how the servant fell on his knees before the king and asked for mercy. The word for the mercy he requested always refers to an extension of time, a delay.[4] The servant's request was essentially, *just be patient with me – extend the promissory note – and I will repay you everything.*

In what can only be described as a display of extravagant, merciful grace, Jesus went on to explain how the king forgave the servant's debt, canceling it completely. While this is precisely what God in His grace has done for each one of His children through Christ's death on the cross, this magnificent truth often fails to penetrate our hearts and minds. Such was the case with this servant; his response to the king's grace was appalling. His immediate response was to go to a fellow-servant who owed him a smaller, reasonable amount. Even though he too asked for mercy, for an extension of time, the servant who had been so lavishly blessed and completely released from his debt, had his fellow-servant thrown into the debtor's prison until he paid back what he owed.

As Jesus continued, He explained how the king then said, "You wicked slave; I forgave you all that debt because you pleaded with me. Should you not also have had mercy on your fellow slave in the same way that I had mercy on you? (Matthew 18:32-33) As readers of Jesus' story, our answer to the king's question is a resounding YES! How could we who have received such extravagant mercy and grace fail to show the same to those who wrong us?

History reveals that Simon Peter never forgot the lesson Jesus taught him about loving forgiveness. It seems almost certain that Peter had Jesus' story in his thoughts when he wrote in his first epistle: "Above all, keep fervent in your love for one another because love covers a multitude of sins" (I Peter 4:8). The word Peter used for a *multitude* is identical to the one used in Hebrews 11 to refer to the *multitude* of Abraham's descendants whom God promised would be like the stars in the heavens, and as the sand on the seashore.

Yes, we are called to practice *seventy times seven – love covers a multitude of sins* type of forgiveness, as our two *one another* verses for this chapter make emphatically clear. Being completely and eternally forgiven by our Lord is given in the New Testament as the basis for forgiving one another. "Be kind to one another, tender-hearted, forgiving each other, *just as God in Christ has forgiven you*" (Ephesians 4:32; italics mine). "Bearing with one another, and forgiving each other, whoever has a complaint against anyone, *just as the Lord forgave you, so also should you*" (Colossians 3:13; italics mine).

As we know from life and Scripture, each one of us will at some point be faced with the question of whether to forgive someone who has deeply hurt or wronged us. Perhaps you are wrestling with this question even as you are reading these words. In the earlier part of the chapter where Jesus answered Peter's question about how often to forgive his brother, Jesus said, "It is inevitable but that offenses are going to come" (Matthew 18:7), and we know this to be true. He also went on to speak of the seriousness of being the offender.

If we are the one offended, however, which is the focus of this chapter, the one who wounded us may come seeking forgiveness, but often they will not. In either case, our calling is to forgive, even as Jesus once said, "And when you stand praying, forgive, if you have anything against anyone" (Mark 11:25). To forgive even when the offender has not asked is wonderfully illustrated in Jesus when He was on the cross, "Father, forgive them for they know not what they are doing" (Luke 23:34).

As we prayerfully reflect on additional applications, I want us to consider some of the harmful consequences of failing to forgive.

First, *a failure to forgive creates a barrier in our relationship with God.* Some would ask how this can be since Christians are already completely justified, forgiven, and clothed in the righteousness of Christ? This is the grand truth Paul explains in Romans, "Therefore, having been justified by faith, we have peace with God through our Lord Jesus Christ" (Romans 5:1). Justification is a legal term describing an accomplished fact, the result being, "There is therefore now no condemnation for those who are in Christ" (Romans 8:1).

Why then are we as Christians to continue to confess our sins, as John explained to the believers in his first epistle: "If we confess our sins, He is faithful and just to *forgive* us our sins, and to cleanse us from all unrighteousness" (I John 1:9). The answer is that even though we are *judicially forgiven*, when we sin as believers, including failing to forgive, our Heavenly Father is, nevertheless, grieved. In the verses immediately preceding his command to forgive one another even as Christ has forgiven us, Paul writes, "Do not grieve

110

the Holy Spirit of God, by whom you were sealed to the day of redemption" (Ephesians 4:30).

The best way to describe what seems to be a paradox is to see that *"judicial forgiveness* is the forgiveness God grants as Judge. This is the forgiveness that was purchased by the atonement Christ rendered on our behalf. But the forgiveness we seek as His children is the *parental forgiveness* God grants as our Father. He is grieved when His children sin. The forgiveness of justification takes care of judicial guilt, but it does not nullify His Fatherly displeasure over our sin."[5] When sin occurs in the lives of God's children, He lovingly disciplines us (not a punishment), but a loving, corrective discipline to train us as His children, making us more and more like Jesus, including being able to forgive one another as He has forgiven us.

Second, *a failure to forgive makes us more vulnerable to Satan's attacks.* In the earlier part of Paul's relational instruction to the church at Ephesus, Paul writes, "Be angry and yet do not sin, and do not let the sun go down on your anger, and do not give the devil an opportunity" (Ephesians 4:26-27). When relational conflicts arise, anger is often present as well. But as we see here, anger does not have to lead to sin. The principle is to keep short accounts, to not let the sun go down on our wrath, but seek to work things through quickly so reconciliation can occur. If we think back to Sue and Wilbur in our opening story, Sue not only allowed the sun to go down on her wrath; she let 13 years of sunsets go down on her lack of forgiveness, which had progressively turned into resentment, and deep-rooted bitterness.

God's alternative to an unforgiving spirit is grace: "See to it that none of you fails to respond to the grace God gives, lest there spring up in you a root of bitterness which not only destroys you but also poisons the lives of many others" (Hebrews 12:15 J. B. Phillips).[6] The picture here is of grace being available for those times when we are hurt, grace that enables us to forgive and not become bitter, poisoning others with our vindictive spirit.

Third, *a failure to forgive blocks our fellowship with the one who offended us, and with other believers as well.* Sadly, most Christians know this from experience. When we fail to forgive our spouse, our children, our parents, or a brother or sister in Christ, a barrier is created in the relationship. We can go through the motions, pretending everything is fine, but the freedom and warmth of fellowship God intends for us to experience is lacking.

One of the great passions expressed by the Apostle John in his first epistle was fellowship, true *koinonia*, originating with God and then with one another. "What we have seen and heard we proclaim to you, so that you too may have fellowship with us; and indeed our fellowship is with the Father, and with His Son, Jesus Christ (I John 1:3). John goes on to explain how this fellowship is maintained: "If we say we have fellowship with Him and yet walk in darkness, we lie and do not practice the truth; but if we walk in the light as He is in the light, we have fellowship with one another, and the blood of His Son, Jesus Christ, keeps us clean from all sin" (I John 1:6-7). This reaffirms what we saw earlier, namely, fellowship is not mere social activity; it is a deeply spiritual exchange between those who are walking in the light, never allowing an unforgiving spirit to come between them.

We move now from the harmful consequences of an unforgiving spirit to some of the rewarding results of forgiving even as Christ has forgiven us.

First, *we take the first essential step toward reconciling a broken relationship.* Forgiveness, while vitally important, is not the same as reconciliation and for this reason; two people are involved. Even if you forgive, the other person may not even be aware that he or she has hurt you. It is also possible that they are fully aware of it, but have no intention of acknowledging that they did anything wrong. The painful reality is that they may never come seeking your forgiveness. Even so, when we forgive, we have taken that all-important first step, making sure our heart is clear before the Lord and toward the offending person, opening the door for complete reconciliation, which we pray will occur.

My wife, Linda, is a spiritually mature follower of Christ, one who seeks to be sensitive to the Lord and obedient to His word. On two occasions in her life, she was deeply hurt by different people, and in both instances, struggled greatly to forgive. Even though Linda was praying about it daily, she found it difficult to let go of her hurt. In time, however, in both instances, she was able to respond to God's grace and forgive. Interestingly, in neither case did the offending persons ever acknowledge their wrong or ask for forgiveness. But because of the forgiveness in Linda's heart, she had taken the first step toward reconciliation, as Scripture describes: "If possible, so far as it depends on you, be at peace with all men" (Romans 12:15). Even though there was never any acknowledgment on the part of the offending persons, Linda's heart remains free.

Second, when we forgive, *we reveal to others the power of Christ to completely transform our entire disposition.* What is so enlightening about our two primary *one another* passages for this chapter (Ephesians 4 and Colossians 3), is that a forgiving heart is but one of several positive virtues the Lord Jesus Christ brings into our lives; He transforms our entire disposition and temperament.

In Ephesians, we read, "Let all bitterness and wrath and anger and clamor and slander be put away from you, along with all malice. Be kind to one another, tenderhearted, forgiving each other, just as God in Christ has forgiven you" (Ephesians 4:31-32). In other words, once we become a new creation in Christ, we put off the self-centered, fleshly way of relating which we previously followed. Now, as a new creation in Christ, one who is ever-changing because of the Holy Spirit's ongoing work in our lives, we become kind and tender-hearted, and quick to forgive. We are not like the unforgiving servant who was still collecting debts even though the king had forgiven him for an impossible amount. Now, as His new creation, we display a Christlike attitude, even toward those who wrong us.

We also see this complete change of character in the relational passage from Colossians: "And so, as those who have been chosen by God, put on a heart of compassion, kindness, humility, gentleness, and patience, bearing with one another and forgiving each other; whoever has a complaint against anyone, just as the Lord forgave you, so also should you. And beyond all these things, put on love which is the perfect bond of unity" (Colossians 3:12-14). This entire paragraph speaks not only of forgiveness but of an entirely new Christlike disposition because of the transforming power of the gospel in our lives. In this passage, forgiveness is described in the present tense, conveying that forgiveness for God's children is to be a way of life.

When we forgive, we reveal to others the power of Christ to completely transform us. These changes are not because of our fleshly determination, but by the miraculous work of Christ. Robin Mark expresses it beautifully in one of his songs, "Lord, Your mercy is so great, that you look beyond our weakness, making purest gold from miry clay, turning sinners into saints."[7]

Third, *we demonstrate our gratitude to God for the gracious, complete forgiveness we have received from Him.* The word for forgiveness used by the Apostle Paul in both Ephesians and Colossians is the same as utilized earlier in Colossians to refer to the forgiveness we have received from God. "When you were dead in your transgressions...He made you alive with Him, having *forgiven* us all our transgressions, having canceled out the certificate of debt consisting of decrees against us, which was hostile to us; and He has taken it out of the way, having nailed it to the cross" (Colossians 2:13-14 Italics mine). The Greek word for forgiveness has within it the word *Charis*, the word for grace. It means *to bestow a favor unconditionally, to treat someone better than they deserve, to freely give good instead of evil.*

What wonderful news this is! During the years at our church in Indianapolis, we would often sing a simple but profound worship chorus with these words: *"He paid a debt He did not owe; I owed a debt I could not pay; I needed someone to take my sins away; and now I sing a brand new song, amazing grace all day long; my Jesus paid a debt that I could never pay."*[8] The words remind us of the servant in Jesus' story whose enormous debt was completely forgiven by the gracious king, even as ours has been forgiven by God. This is the extravagant, undeserving, gracious forgiveness we are to give to those who wrong us.

Fourth, *we display to a watching world the definitive mark by which Christians are to be known.* Immediately following Paul's words in Ephesians – "forgiving one another just as God in Christ has forgiven you" - we read, "Therefore, be imitators of God, as beloved children, and walk in love, just as Christ loved you, and gave Himself up for us, an offering and sacrifice to God as a fragrant aroma" (Ephesians 5:1-2). We are never more like God than when we forgive!

Chapter Nine Discussion Questions

1. In the story of Sue and Wilbur, how was her attitude the opposite of love in I Corinthians 13?
2. What are possible explanations as to why the servant in Jesus' story failed to forgive his fellow servant even after he had been given his extravagant debt?
3. Why is it that those who fail to receive the forgiveness of Christ tend to become *debt collectors*?
4. What is the central biblical truth as to why we are to forgive?
5. According to the author, what is the difference between judicial and parental forgiveness?
6. According to Hebrews 12:15, how does grace come into play when we are hurt and wounded by someone? How is this grace received from God?
7. What is the difference between forgiveness and reconciliation? Can you have one without the other? Why or why not?

Chapter Ten

Be at Peace with One Another

"Salt is good, but if the salt becomes unsalty, with what will you make it salty again? Have salt in yourselves, and be at peace with one another."

Mark 9:50

Peace is one of the prominent themes in the New Testament and is found in every book except I John. Because peace is of such immense value, the Apostle Paul included it as a greeting in many of his epistles, "Grace to you and peace, from God our Father and the Lord Jesus Christ" (Philippians 1:2). God Himself is referred to as the God of all peace (Hebrews 13:20), indicating that He is the source of all true peace.

The Greek word for peace, eirene, conveys the idea of *relational harmony*. The Psalmist captured it perfectly when he wrote, "Behold, how good and how pleasant it is for brothers to dwell together in unity" (Psalm 133:1). Living in unity is possible only when each person is in relational harmony with all the others. This is true in marriage, in the family, and the church. If we are genuine Christians, we will pursue peace in all our relationships. One of the beatitudes given by Jesus at the beginning of His Sermon on the Mount highlights this truth: "Blessed are the peacemakers, for they shall be called the sons of God" (Matthew 5:9). Pursuing peace with every other member of the family of God is fundamental to our Christian character, part of our spiritual DNA.

In contrast to our earlier *one other* commands which were found in the epistles, our focus in this chapter comes from the

117

Gospels, from the lips of Jesus Himself: "Have salt in yourselves and be at peace with one another" (Mark 9:50). What we will see, however, as we progress through our study, is that the command to be at peace is reiterated and reinforced in the various letters to the churches.

As we take a closer look at what Jesus taught about peace, we discover certain statements which, at first glance, appear to be contradictory. For this reason, we must always look at the context to see when, where, and to whom Jesus was speaking. For example, He once said, "Do not think that I came to bring peace to the earth; I did not come to bring peace, but a sword" (Matthew 10:34). Based on the many positive things He said about peace, this does not sound like Jesus. But let us allow Him to continue so He can make His point: "For I came to set a man against his father, and a daughter against her mother, and a daughter in law against her mother in law; and a man's enemies will be those of his own household" (Matthew 10:35-36; Micah 7:6).

Jesus was instructing His disciples before sending them out on a preaching mission, preparing them to be realistic in their expectations. While the ultimate end of the gospel is peace, the reality is that it often divides. After making His startling statement, Jesus expanded on His comment by quoting a passage from the Minor Prophet, Micah. Well-informed Jews understood that when the Messiah eventually came, there would be a relational sword of division, even in the family. Jesus was not saying that He came to poison family relationships, but He was declaring that when He comes into a home, a sword of division, though often painful, is inevitable. Anytime there is a divided response to the truth of the Gospel, relational disharmony is often the outcome and not peace.

What is striking is how Jesus experienced this sorrowful reality in His own family. While His mother, Mary, believed in Him, as did His legal father, Joseph, other family members did not. The

Apostle John states, "Not even His brothers were believing in Him" (John 7:5). This sword of division was a reality in His Nazareth home. This would change following His crucifixion and resurrection, as the New Testament reveals, but Jesus knew firsthand this relational pain of division.

It is one I encountered in the early months of my Christian life, and it may be a trial some who are reading these words are experiencing even now. Knowing that Jesus went through this difficulty reminds me of these encouraging words: "We do not have a high priest who cannot sympathize with our weaknesses, but One who has been tempted in all things as we are, yet without sin. Therefore, let us draw near with confidence to the throne of grace, that we may receive mercy and find grace to help in time of need" (Hebrews 4:15-16). Whatever our struggle, even if it is this sword of division with loved ones, we have a High Priest who understands, and who also provides mercy and grace sufficient for the challenge.

In contrast, is our key verse for this chapter. Jesus is again speaking to His disciples but, in this instance, He is instructing them about their relationship with one another. "Have salt in yourselves, and be at peace with one another" (Mark 9:50). To appreciate His illustration, we must remember that when Jesus was conducting His ministry, life was much like it is today in third world countries. Being unable to purify salt as we do in our country, along with other items like sugar, flour, meal, etc., bugs and other contaminants could easily enter it, rendering it unusable. In the opening words of His Sermon on the Mount, Jesus had said to His disciples, "You are the salt of the earth, but if the salt becomes tasteless, how can it be made salty again? It is no longer good for anything, except to be thrown out and trampled underfoot by men" (Matthew 5:13).

In our central verse for this chapter, Jesus returns to this same analogy, commanding His followers to have salt in themselves and be at peace with one another. His point is that if they indeed had *salt in themselves*, they would demonstrate their character as His disciples by being at peace with one another.

As we turn from Jesus' initial command about peace, we move ahead several years to additional words on this theme written by His apostles to the churches. By this time, the church had spread from Jerusalem, Judea, and Samaria, and out to the Gentile world. Before the birth of the church, the racial divisions within society ran deep. When we include the separation between masters and slaves, even among men and women, the unity in the church could only be described as miraculous. In Paul's epistle to the church of Galatia, he wrote these astonishing words: "You are all sons of God through faith in Christ. For all of you who were baptized into Christ have clothed yourselves with Christ. There is neither Jew nor Greek, there is neither slave nor free man, there is neither male nor female; for you are all one in Christ Jesus" (Galatians 3:26-28).

How did this inexplicable, relational unity come about? *First, this reality of peace came about because Christ broke down all the walls that had divided people.* In Paul's letter to the church at Ephesus, a congregation made up primarily of Gentiles, he reminded them of their lost, hopeless condition before Christ. "Remember that formerly you, the Gentiles according to the flesh...remember that at that time you were separate from Christ, excluded from the commonwealth of Israel, and strangers to the covenants of promise, having no hope and without God in the world (Ephesians 2:11-12). What a desperate condition they were in, and that includes us, since most who are reading these words are not Jews by nationality, but Gentiles. But Paul explains how this miraculous peace came about: "But now in Christ Jesus you who formerly were far off have been brought near by the blood of Christ. For *He Himself is our peace*, who has made both groups into one, and broke down the barrier of the dividing wall...so that in Himself He might make the two into one new man, thus *establishing peace*...and might reconcile them both into one body through the cross..." (Ephesians 2:13-16; italics mine)

What we see is that Jesus Himself, and what He accomplished on the cross through His blood, is the basis of our peace. That was true in the first-century church, and it remains true today. But Paul was not finished: "And He came and preached *peace* to you who were far away, and *peace* to those who were near; for through Him we both have access in one Spirit to the Father. So then, you are no longer strangers and aliens, but you are fellow citizens with the saints, and are of God's household" (Ephesians 2:18-19).

Just as Jesus was the basis for peace in the diverse, first-century church, so He is in our racially divided culture today. During our times of relational stress with other believers, we must always come back to Jesus Himself, the permanent basis of our peace.

There was a second component to their peace - *the unchanging truths that unite all true believers.* In this same letter to the Ephesians, Paul moves from Christ Himself and His blood, to seven unchanging, truths. "Be diligent to preserve the unity of the Spirit in the bonds of peace. There is one body and one Spirit, just as you were also called in one hope of your calling; one Lord, one faith, one baptism, one God and Father of all, who is over all and through all and in all" (Ephesians 4:3-6). Note that Paul's admonition had nothing to do with achieving unity, but rather to preserving (maintaining) the unity Jesus had already secured, one that is ours *in the bonds of peace.* The word picture for a *bond of peace* is of a loving, spiritual cord that surrounds and binds the church together. Note carefully the seven unchanging truths which unite us: *one body, one Spirit, one hope of our calling, one Lord, one faith, one baptism, and one God and Father of all who is over all and through all and in all!* While there will always be differences between Christians, these unchanging, non-negotiable truths are meant to unite us. When combined with what Jesus accomplished through His blood on the cross, we have an objective basis for relational harmony and *being at peace with one another.*

In the remainder of this chapter, I want to highlight some application points I like to refer to as – *the things which make for peace.* We will see this phrase in one of the applications, but it has its origin in the life of Jesus Himself. "When He approached the city, He wept over it saying, 'If you had known in this day *the things which make for peace!* But now they are hidden from your eyes" (Luke 19:41-42; italics mine). In reflecting on His ministry, Jesus was deeply sorrowful that the people of Jerusalem missed their opportunity to know the peace He came to give, but by that time it was too late. So, what are the truths which make for peace for us as believers?

The first is this: *diligently preserve the unity of the Spirit and the peace God has given us.* "Be diligent (make every effort) to preserve (maintain) the unity of the Spirit in the bond of peace" (Ephesians 4:3). As those who are bound together with Christ in the unity of the Spirit, in practical terms, how are we to preserve it?

For one thing, we must make harmonious relationships a much higher priority than many of us are doing. Because of our lack of tact and insensitivity, it is easy to say or do something that deeply wounds a brother or sister in Christ. We may sense at the time that what we did injured them, but all too often our tendency is to minimize our wrong and do nothing to make things right.

A frequently overlooked teaching of Jesus addresses this point: "Everyone who is angry with his brother shall be guilty before the court, and everyone who says, 'you good for nothing,' shall be guilty before the Supreme Court; and whoever says, 'you fool' shall be guilty enough to go to hell" (Matthew 5:22). Strong words for sure, but do you recall what Jesus said next? How does He follow up this piercing warning? "Therefore, if you are presenting your gift at the altar, and there remember that your brother has something against you, leave your offering there before the altar, and go; first be reconciled to your brother, and then come and offer your gift"

(Matthew 5:23). According to Jesus, making peace and pursuing reconciliation with a wounded brother or sister is of far greater importance than ceremoniously participating in an act of worship. Putting into practice this action described by Jesus is a tangible way of being diligent to preserve the unity of the Spirit in the bonds of peace! It comes down to how much we value our relationships, and how serious we are to obey God's word.

Second, *pursue the things which make for peace.* Here we come to the identical phrase used by Jesus when He wept over the city: "So then, let us pursue *the things which make for peace*, and the building up of one another" (Romans 14:19; italics mine). The context was that older, more mature believers were passing judgment on those who were younger in the faith; their attitude was creating a stumbling block. Paul corrected them by pointing out that their attitude was not an expression of the Christlike love for which His followers were to be known. In the little phrase, "so then," he is urging them to turn from the judgmental attitude, which was causing their younger brothers to stumble, to an attitude of not putting a stumbling block in another's way. The higher and more loving way of relating was to *pursue the things which make for peace, for the building up of one another.* The alternative to critical, judgmental remarks is to seek to build up and edify one another.

Third, *do everything within your power to live in peace with everyone.* The Apostle Paul's admonition is clear: "If possible, in as much as it depends on you, be at peace with all men" (Romans 12:18). This verse is linked to Jesus' command in the Gospels, with the wording essentially the same in the Greek language. As a way of life, we who are Christ's followers are to pursue peace. This means prayerfully searching our hearts to see if we have sinned, and if so, going quickly to confess that sin and humbly asking for forgiveness. We have no control as to whether the wounded person will forgive us or not; the key is doing everything within our power, as much as it depends on us, to be at peace.

It is amazing how quickly a broken relationship can change when one person humbly and truthfully deals with his or her sin, instead of pointing out where the other person was wrong. Jesus taught the necessity of this in His Sermon on the Mount: "How can you say to your brother, 'Let me take the speck out of your eye,' and behold the log that is in your own eye. You hypocrite; *first* take the log out of your own eye, and then you will see clearly to take the speck out of your brother's eye" (Matthew 7:4-5).

In my more than 50 years as a pastor, I can recall deeply troubled relationships that were healed, simply because one person was willing to humbly confess his part of the conflict. The opposite is also true; relationships that could have been reconciled remained broken because of pride, stubbornness, self-will, or lack of forgiveness. Our culture, at times the church as well, is quick to explain away conflicts by putting them in that convenient category we call *irreconcilable differences.* My assertion, however, is that when we follow God's Word and depend on Him, even the deepest conflicts can be resolved. This is because God has given to us the *word and ministry of reconciliation* (II Corinthians 5:18-19; italics mine). Following His Word and prayerfully depending on His Spirit can lead to *reconcilable differences*, and when this happens, God is glorified!

The fourth truth is closely related: *make sure that your relational attitudes are pleasing to the Lord.* So often we focus on the horizontal, on the person with whom we have the conflict, rather than prayerfully searching our hearts before the Lord. In the wonderful Psalm which speaks of God's omniscience, His omnipresence, and His omnipotence, King David concludes with this prayer: "Search me, O God, and know my heart; try me and know my ways, and see if there be any hurtful way in me, and lead me in the everlasting way" (Psalm 139:23-24).

When we sincerely pray in this way, asking God to enable us to search our hearts, and with the intent of following through on what He reveals to us, miraculous things happen. This is because God is pleased with our desire to pursue peace in all our relationships. Consider this wonderful truth from Proverbs: "When a man's (or woman's) ways please the Lord, He makes even his enemies be at peace with him" (Proverbs 16:7).

As I have spoken at funerals and memorial services over the years, I have at times witnessed the deep regret in bereaved family members who were not at peace with the person who died. Often it was a son or daughter who had failed to make peace with their mother or father. While it is possible to ask God for forgiveness for wrongs that were done, the opportunity has passed to make peace with the one who died. In witnessing this on more occasions than I can recall, my prayer has been that God will enable me to be one who pursues the things which make for peace in all my relationships. I hope you are doing the same.

Chapter Ten Discussion Questions

1. The author writes of peacemaking being part of the Christian's DNA. What does he give as the biblical basis for this statement?

2. What are the implications of Jesus growing up in a home without complete relational harmony, having brothers who did not believe in Him? How did this prepare Him for His ministry as our Great High Priest?

3. What are the two overarching certainties in Scripture that are the basis for our peace as believers?

4. What are some practical things we can do to preserve the unity of the Spirit more diligently in the bonds of peace?

5. How can we pursue the things which make for relational peace within the Body of Christ?

6. Some seeking peace will only say, "I'm sorry," and the issue is not resolved. What are some reasons why it is important to specifically state where you were wrong and then ask, "Would you forgive me?"

7. Discuss the truths in Proverbs 16:7 about peacemaking. What does it say about our part - and God's part?

Chapter Eleven
Admonish One Another

"And concerning you, my brethren, I myself also am convinced that you yourselves are full of goodness, filled with all knowledge, and able also to admonish one another."

Romans 15:14

In 1970, Jay Adams, viewed by many as the father of biblical counseling, authored a ground-breaking book entitled *Competent to Counsel.* In it, he coined a phrase called *nouthetic counseling, nouthetic* coming from the Greek word *noutheteo,* most often translated in the New Testament as - *to admonish.* [1] A pivotal verse in his instructive book is the central focus for this chapter: "And concerning you, my brethren, I myself also am convinced that you yourselves are full of goodness, filled with all knowledge, and able to admonish one another" (Romans 15:14). While *admonish one another* is not an actual command, but a participle linked to Paul's commendation to the church at Rome, namely, that they were *able to admonish,* it is nevertheless an important element in our *one-another* ministry and life together in the church.

An enlightening insight into the essence of this word is when the Apostle Paul was addressing the fathers in his letter to the church at Ephesus: "Fathers, do not exasperate your children, but bring them up in the nurture and *admonition* of the Lord" (Ephesians 6:4; italics mine). To admonish is inherent in our calling as parents; we admonish our children because we love them and want to protect them from every form of danger. It will not always be pleasant for them to receive, or easy for us to give, but admonition is for their safety, training, and future welfare.

To admonish is also one of the responsibilities in our life together as believers. While this is clear in God's Word, the thought is frightening to many, though some gladly embrace the idea. A few even believe that to admonish others is their gift or calling in the church when it may be nothing more than self-justification for their critical spirit. Even with the fears and potential abuses, when admonition is done with the right motive and proper attitude, and following the guidelines of Scripture, it has the potential to be one of the most loving actions we can take toward another believer, or from them to us. The writer of Proverbs states, "Better is open rebuke than love that is concealed. Faithful are the words of a friend" (Proverbs 27:5-6). Even with the benefits, the command to admonish one another is not among the most popular, which may explain why it is not practiced at all in many churches.

Noutheteo is one of several Greek words with no exact English equivalent. The NASB translates it as to *admonish*, as we have seen. Other renderings include to counsel, to correct, to instruct, and to put sense into. Gene Getz points out, "The word *noutheteo* does not refer to casual communication or normal-type preaching. It implies a definite exhortation, correction, and warning."[2]

As we look at this truth more carefully, we see, *first, that this type of admonition presumes a specific need in the one to be admonished.* A Christian has a problem, sin, or an obstacle that needs to be faced and overcome; something is wrong and he or she needs admonition.

If we are simply instructing or teaching a believer, the Greek word is *didasko,* which describes the communication of information to a person or group with clarity, understanding, and in a way that is memorable.[3] The majority of my ministry as a pastor on Sunday mornings is *didasko,* though there are often elements of admonition in my sermons.

In contrast, *noutheteo* always presupposes a need for change in the person being admonished. What often makes this difficult is that the brother or sister in need may not be aware of the problem. Even when the problem is recognized, the person may not be receptive, especially when approached by someone coming for the express purpose of admonishing.

On the other hand, some are keenly aware of their need and so motivated to face it that a trusted friend or confidant may be sought out for biblical counseling. Whether in a formal counseling session or an informal private meeting of one believer with another, the goal of the admonisher is to be God's fellow worker in bringing about biblical change.

Second, this type of admonition presumes verbal assistance rooted in Scripture. Not only is there a problem to be addressed; a solution is available in God's Word. This is the good news to be communicated from the admonisher to the one in need. This may take place in a more formal setting such as the office of the counselor, but it may also occur in a more informal gathering of one believer with another who is, as Paul stated, *able to admonish,* or *competent to counsel.*

One of the profound promises of the sufficiency of Scripture is that "God has given to us everything pertaining to life and godliness through the true knowledge of Him who called us by His own glory and excellence" (II Peter 1:3). An immature admonisher may exhort his or her friend based on personal convictions, but not biblical in what he communicated. The crucial action that is needed to bring liberating truth to the person in need is for God's Word to be spoken lovingly.

Thirdly, this type of admonition presumes a loving motive that seeks only God's best for the one being admonished. If this essential element is missing, our admonition will be in vain. The truth we speak must always be for the benefit of the one we are admonishing, and we convey this by "speaking the truth in love" (Ephesians 4:15).

In looking at the admonitions recorded in Scripture, love is always prominent. One tender example is when the Apostle Paul was admonishing the immature, divided church in Corinth. "I do not write these things to shame you but *to admonish you* as my beloved children. For if you were to have countless tutors in Christ, yet you would not have many fathers, for in Christ Jesus I became your father through the Gospel" (I Corinthians 4:14-15; Italics mine). While Paul's admonition to the church was strong and direct, his motive was clear. His intent was not to embarrass, to expose, or to bring shame; he was doing what any good father would do with his children, and the Corinthians were Paul's spiritual children. His loving, protective heart for them is preeminent in his admonition.

An even more poignant example is when Jesus admonished Simon Peter following his denial. In the hours leading up to the cross, Peter had boasted, "Even if I have to die with you, I will not deny you" (Matthew 26:35). Jesus, however, knew Peter better than he knew himself, and had previously explained, "Truly I say to you that this very night, before a rooster crows, you will deny Me three times" (Matthew 26:34). After his shameful denial, "Peter went out and wept bitterly" (Matthew 26:75). He was immediately in deep remorse, needing forgiveness, but also to be lovingly admonished. Fully aware of this, one of Jesus' initial appearances in the hours following His resurrection was to Peter. (See I Corinthians 15:3-5)

The example I want to highlight came some days later when Jesus appeared to seven of his disciples, graciously preparing breakfast for them after a frustrating night of fishing when they caught nothing. Jesus, yet unidentified, called out to them from the shore, saying, "Cast your net on the right-hand side of the boat, and you will find a catch.' So, they cast, and then they were not able to haul it in because of the great number of fish" (John 21:6). At this point John called out to Peter, informing him that the stranger on the shore was Jesus. Consistent with his impetuous personality, "Peter put on his outer garment, for he was stripped for work, and threw himself into the sea" (John 21:7). What a memorable breakfast that must have been for each one of them!

It was after they completed the meal when Jesus began to gently *admonish* and lovingly restore Peter to his calling. He began by asking, "Do you love me more than these?" (John 21:15) It is not clear from the text if Jesus referred to the other disciples, or the boat and the fishing nets. As a result, we cannot be sure who or what Jesus was referring to in the word *these.* What we know for sure is that His question was the beginning of loving admonition to His impulsive but cherished apostle.

Peter, now a more humble and realistic man following his denials, responded by affirming that he had a strong, brotherly affection for Jesus. You are likely are familiar with the account of how Jesus asked Peter three times if he loved Him, providing Peter with three opportunities to affirm his love, a number corresponding to his shameful denials. After each response, Jesus said to him, "Feed My lambs...Tend My sheep...Feed My sheep" (John 21:15-17). Each command was designed to clarify Peter's future calling, one he would fulfill in his ministry to the church. Jesus continued, "When you were younger you used to gird yourself and walk wherever you wished; but when you grow old, you will stretch out your hands and someone else will gird you, and bring you where you do not wish to go.' Now, this He said signifying by what kind of death Peter would glorify God. And when He had said this, He said to him 'Follow Me'" (John 21:18-19).

As we know from the book of Acts and Peter's two New Testament Epistles, Peter recovered and went on in the power of the Holy Spirit to play a major role in the first-century church. The loving admonition by Jesus produced the intended effect. When the time comes for us to admonish a struggling brother or sister, my prayer is that our loving, biblical counsel can be as effective.

In the final part of this chapter, I want to turn further toward application by asking four questions for potential admonishers, each one rising out of God's Word. The first two come from our key verse for this chapter: "And concerning you, my brothers, I myself am convinced that you yourselves are full of goodness, filled with all knowledge, and able also to admonish one another" (Romans 15:14).

The first is obvious from the text: *Is your lifestyle marked by spiritual goodness?* Paul was convinced that there were people in the church at Rome who were *full of goodness.* This word for *goodness* is the same as in Galatians 5:22-23 where Paul lists the fruit of the Spirit, one being *goodness.* This is not a quality we have naturally, but only by the fruit of the Spirit and His transforming work in our lives. It describes not only one's character but how our character expresses itself in relationships. In his *Expository Dictionary of New Testament Words,* W. E. Vine states: "It is not only good as a quality but also goodness in action, goodness expressing itself in deeds."[4] Being one of the biblical qualifications which make us *competent to counsel* and admonish biblically, an appropriate question is if our lifestyle, particularly in how we relate to people, seeking to serve them, is marked by this Spirit-produced goodness.

Barnabas is a New Testament character loved by everyone, his name meaning "Son of Encouragement" (Acts 4:36). When Gentiles were beginning to respond to the Gospel and flood into the church, the elders in Jerusalem could think of no better person to encourage them than Barnabas. "Then, when he arrived and witnessed the grace of God, he rejoiced and began to encourage them all with resolute heart to remain true to the Lord, for *he was a good man*, full of the Holy Spirit and faith" (Acts 11:23-24; italics mine). The goodness in Barnabas, produced by the Holy Spirit, was expressed in how he related to people, treating them with honor, even those who were vastly different from his fellow Jews. This relational quality of being full of goodness must be prominent in our lives if we aspire to be a biblical counselor and admonisher.

The second question also comes from Romans 15:14, and it is this: *Do you have a good working knowledge of the Scriptures?* In addition to being *full of goodness,* Paul also stated that they were *filled with all knowledge.* The MacArthur Study Bible explains: "This refers to deep, intimate knowledge indicating that the Roman believers were doctrinally sound, illustrating the fact that truth and virtue are inseparable."[6]

This does not mean one has to know the Bible perfectly as there is always more to learn and understand as we diligently study the Scriptures. What it does mean is that biblical counseling and admonition is not for novices; it is for those who are well established in their faith and possess a good working knowledge of the Scriptures.

In the early 1970s, my wife and I were involved in Campus Crusade for Christ, working with college students in San Jose, California. A leader I respected made a statement that marked my life from that point forward. He said, "When someone asks a question, I try to always follow the *open book policy.*" He explained that if we are to be a source of spiritual assistance to others, we must give them more than our thoughts. We must be able to *open the book*, giving them counsel and admonition from God's Word. Being *filled with all knowledge* means having an ability to let others know what God's Word has to say, whatever the topic.

The third question is this: *Do you have the spiritual discernment to understand when admonition is the appropriate action?* As we relate to one another in the church, we will encounter people with a wide range of needs. At times, an admonition is precisely what is needed, but it is not always the appropriate action, as we see in the Apostle Paul's instruction in his first letter to the church at Thessalonica. "Admonish the unruly, encourage the fainthearted, help the weak, be patient with all men (I Thessalonians 5:14). Paul identifies people with different types of problems: the unruly, the weak, and the fainthearted, each one needing a different expression of love.

The unruly, for example, is one who has a problem submitting to authority, likely to the rule and authority of God's Word. Because of the grave danger in failing to take God's Word seriously, this person is one who needs to be admonished.

On the other hand, some in the church are simply weak. Exhausted Christians do not need admonition but for a caring, roll up your sleeve's kind of brother or sister in Christ willing to come alongside to provide practical assistance.

The third group Paul identifies is the fainthearted. To admonish a fainthearted person would likely crush them and add to their discouragement; this person's need is for encouragement.

Interestingly, Paul concludes this brief but enlightening instruction by adding, "Be patient with all men." Even the unruly person needs patience from his or her admonishers, as do those who are weak and fainthearted. Regardless of the problem, everyone needs patience, as Paul makes clear: "Be patient with all men" (I Thessalonians 5:14).

Fourthly, will you take prayerful precautions to make sure that your admonition is done at the right time and best place? This admonition is rarely if ever to be done in public. Jesus gave careful instruction about this issue: "If your brother sins, go and show him his fault in private; if he listens to you, you have won your brother"

(Matthew 18:15). Though one or two others are to become involved if a brother or sister in sin does not respond positively, and even the church, (See Matthew 18:16-17), the goal is never to expose, but to win and see the erring one brought to repentance.

There have been times in my ministry when someone in the church needed to be admonished. In my fear, I was tempted to admonish that person in a sermon (without calling names) instead of courageously and lovingly going to him privately as God's Word instructs. This is not to say that admonition is never appropriate in a sermon, for it is often necessary when one is faithfully exegeting the Biblical text.

Our times of corporate worship also include teaching and admonition, but not for the sake of only one person. We see this in Paul's instruction to the churches of Colossae: "Let the word of Christ richly dwell within you, with all wisdom teaching and *admonishing* one another with psalms, hymns, and spiritual songs" (Colossians 3:16; italics mine). Here we see that admonition is being given to the church, even in the music we sing.

As a pastor who is nearing the end of my 8th decade of life, there have been times when I have admonished others, and occasions when others have admonished me. Some of the admonition has been successful, and at other times not so much. To admonish biblically requires wisdom, maturity, and love, along with someone whose heart is receptive to biblical truth.

The admonition I will always treasure came in late spring of 1970 when a friend came to admonish me at the deepest level of my identity as a husband, father, and of my ministry. After speaking gracious, complimentary words to me as he was advancing me into a new position of leadership in campus ministry, he then said, "However...", and paused for a moment; I wondered what could be coming next. He continued by saying, "I know you will respond to what I am about to say to you because of this verse in Proverbs:

'Rebuke a wise man and he will love you. Give instruction to a wise man and he will be still wiser; teach a righteous man and he will increase in learning'" (Proverbs 9:8-9). Even though I was apprehensive, I was intrigued by what he was going to say.

Simply put, his words were these: "Tom, my impression is that you are putting the ministry ahead of your marriage and your calling as a father. If this is true, the time will come when you no longer have a ministry, and you no longer have a marriage or family."

While my initial impulse was to defend and justify myself, rationalizing away what he had said, I chose not to do so. After all, he had referred to me as *a wise and righteous man*! What I would later come to see was that his admonition was part of God's sovereign plan to bring greater health to my marriage and family, and renewed strength and credibility to my ministry.

Only a few weeks later, as part of our summer training, Linda and I heard for the first time straightforward, biblical teaching on marriage and family from Dr. Howard Hendricks of Dallas Seminary, two weeks in length. About halfway through the second week, in response to the Holy Spirit's convicting work in my heart; in repentance, I humbled myself and asked Linda's forgiveness for failing to be the husband and father Scripture reveals that I am to be. I also asked for her patience, being aware I could not become overnight the man I knew God was calling me to be. She graciously forgave me, also asking for my forgiveness. That was a lifechanging, new beginning for our marriage, our family, and our ministry. Without that wise, loving admonition from a bold but loving Christian brother, I would not be writing these words today.

Chapter Eleven Discussion Questions

1. The author writes of how admonition can be one of the most loving actions Christians can take toward one another. To what extent have you found this to be true in your experience? Why or why not?

2. What attitudes and actions are required if a Christian needs admonition but is doing nothing to seek help? Describe the approach that should be taken.

3. What does the author mean when he states that a potential admonisher should *have a good working knowledge of the Scriptures?*

4. Read again and discuss the implications of I Thessalonians 5:14. How can we gain wisdom to discern the appropriate action to take when a fellow-believer is hurting.

5. The author tells of a Christian brother who came to confront and admonish him about his role as a husband and father. What marks of wisdom could you detect in the life of his admonisher?

6. Has there been a time in your life when God used someone to admonish you? Describe how that impacted you.

7. What is one application you hope to make based on the truths in this chapter?

Chapter Twelve
Bear with One Another

"Bearing with one another, and forgiving each other, whoever has a complaint against anyone; just as the Lord forgave you, so also should you."

Colossians 3:13

Each time Linda and I return to Wilmore, Kentucky, for class reunions or to visit friends, we love to go to the library steps at Asbury University where I first asked her for a date in the fall of 1960. We met several weeks earlier just before school began, but had no further face to face contact until that decisive day on the library steps. We did have our eyes on one another, I more so than she, to the degree that I commented to a friend who came to visit me on campus, *"Do you see that girl walking down the sidewalk? That is who I am going to marry!"*

My plan on that memorable day at the library was to ask Linda to go with me to the fall Mission's Conference, and the Dean of Student's home afterward for pizza. As I stopped to speak to her on the steps, the sunlight was beaming down on her face, and I noticed a scar over her eye I had not seen before. As I turned to walk away, she also observed something about me she had not witnessed until that moment, a large brown mole on the back of my neck, a birthmark. Neither of us ventured to communicate our observations and thoughts until several months later. Like all who become infatuated, we were completely blind to one another's flaws.

In the 60 years since that landmark day, 57 of them as a married couple, I have learned to *bear with* Linda's flaws, including the scar she received from being hit with a baseball bat as a child, and she has learned to *bear with* the large mole God gave me while still in my mother's womb.

Our more demanding challenges, however, would stem from deeper flaws, ones every married couple has to face: personal weaknesses, different ways of communicating, immensely different backgrounds and ways of looking at life, different priorities, annoying habits, peculiarities, quirks and idiosyncrasies, recurring failures and sins, those times when we fail to walk in the Spirit, our tendency toward self-centeredness, and the list goes on and on. Gene Getz comments, "To *bear with one another* means being patient with each other's weaknesses. Not one of us is perfect. All of us fail, particularly in human relationships. How easy it is to expect more from other Christians than we do from ourselves."[1]

What is interesting in hindsight is that as Linda and I were planning our wedding for July 5, 1963, the biblical passage we chose to have read in the ceremony was Colossians 3:12-17, one of the most comprehensive relational passages in the New Testament. Even today, after nearly six decades, we are continuing to learn what this rich passage means in terms of application, but patiently bearing with one another is at its core.

Learning to bear with one another is essential for any marriage to survive. As I look at our relationship, Linda has needed to bear with me much more than I with her, and I am beyond thankful for the patient grace she personifies. While essential, bearing with one another does not mean avoiding troubling issues and irritations that need to be addressed. Honest communication is required for a marriage to be healthy. The key to healthy, constructive communication (one most tend to overlook), is *to seek to understand more than to be understo*od. When it is time to talk about the difficult issues, we must seek to prayerfully comprehend what the other person is saying without defending ourselves or placing the blame on them. When the time comes for us to speak about the flaws of the other person, we must seek to communicate with kindness and humility, keeping in mind our mutual need for ongoing, forbearing grace.

When we broaden our focus to the entire home, what is true in marriage is true in all family relationships; they cannot thrive without an abundance of forbearance. It is within the home where we come to know one another as in no other social unit, for this is where we share life day after day, week after week, and year after year. We see one another at our best and our worst; this is true of both parents and children.

My experience is that children most always expect more of their parents than they do of any other adult in their lives. Parents are the same, having higher expectations of their own children than those in other families, and part of this is understandable. God is the one who established the family, and in doing so He entrusted parents the task being so overwhelming, it is impossible to succeed without God's wisdom and total dependence on Him. The psalmist summarized it well: "Unless the Lord builds the house, they labor in vain who build it" (Psalm 127:1). Without massive amounts of forbearing grace in every member of the family, the relationships we value so highly can easily be destroyed, and often are.

The same applies to relationships in the church, the family of God. When we become serious about *experiencing the church by embracing the one another's,* our strengths and weaknesses will soon be exposed. On the other hand, when we learn to patiently bear with one another in love, our relationships progress to a considerably deeper level, one approaching the *koinonia* type of fellowship God designed for His family.

Simply stated, the challenge God has placed before us is to *patiently bear with one another in love.* In addressing this issue, Gene Getz again provides this insight: "When we are tempted to be impatient with one another, we need to think about Jesus Christ and His attitude toward us. This was Paul's secret. The Lord's longsuffering and patience marked his life and gave him unusual tolerance toward others."[2]

These are Paul's impactful words: "It is a trustworthy statement, deserving full acceptance, that Christ Jesus came into the world to save sinners, among whom I am foremost of all. Yet for this reason I found mercy, so that in me as the foremost, Jesus Christ might demonstrate His perfect patience as an example for those who would believe in Him for eternal life" (I Timothy 1:15-16). Seeing himself as a recipient of God's love and patience enabled Paul to respond graciously to others throughout his ministry, showing them the identical love and patience he had received. Here again, we come face to face with the relational truth common to the one another's; our calling is to give to one another what we first received from the Lord.

In our journey as God's children on our way to the Father's house, our patience with one another is certain to be tested. One such time for me occurred several years ago in Tyler, Texas. There was a man in the church near my age, and our families were in a similar season of life. Our children were also in school together, and our sons' teammates on the same soccer team. This meant we saw one another frequently, probably more than either of us preferred, because whatever the issue, we were always on opposing sides. To be honest, I found myself praying at times that God would move this man out of town, or at least to a different church.

As the months passed and he was still there, God began to deal with my unloving, unbiblical, and sinful attitude. I was like the member of the body Paul described whose attitude was, "I have no need of you" (I Corinthians 12:21), for this was exactly how I felt. As God continued His work, however, I purposed by His strength to accept this brother who to me was *irregular.* By God's grace, I would

141

seek to value him, treat him with respect, and patiently bear with him when God placed us together. Not surprisingly, because of the lessons God wanted to teach me, it appeared He often arranged for me to be with this difficult man. My perception was that he viewed me as *irregular* as well. My experience is that most of us have someone of this variety in our lives, and we are likely *irregular* to at least one person in our relational circle, if not more.

Years passed, and the time came when God was calling us to say goodbye to the people and ministry we loved in Tyler, moving to Indianapolis to begin a new church, a church plant of Community Church of Greenwood. Soon after announcing our decision, I saw *my friend* at a soccer game. He congratulated me on the move, affirmed his belief that I would do a good job, and then unexpectedly became quite emotional. As we sat by one another on the bleachers, he put his arm around me, and with tears in his eyes he said with sincere emotion, *"Tom, while you and I have not always seen things eye to eye, as the years have passed I have come to view you as one of my very best friends!"* While I did not view him at that level of friendship, my brother in Christ sensed that I had sought to relate to him with grace. After our conversation I thanked God for enabling me to extend to him the forbearance and love I had failed to show in the early months of our relationship.

None of us can foresee the future and the myriad of ways our patience and forbearance with one another will be tested. One unforgettable example that made a deep impression on me is of a mature Christian lady in our church in Indiana who cared for her aging mother for the final five years of her life. What made her task so daunting was that her mother had Alzheimer's, meaning that she could not recognize her daughter during that entire period, and constantly complained that she was not being cared for adequately. Nevertheless, her daughter continued to *patiently bear* with her mother that entire time, embracing God's calling for her.

Because God perfectly understands how relationships work and how difficult they can be for His children, He prompted the Apostle Paul through the Holy Spirit to instruct and admonish us with "gentleness and patience, bearing with one another in love" (Colossians 3:12-13).

Like many Greek words, *to bear or forebear* is difficult to fully capture with one English word. Several Greek words have different shades of meaning, depending on their context and what they are describing. As an example, W.E. Vine, in his *Expository Dictionary of New Testament Words,* makes a distinction between *hupomone,* which expresses patience regarding adverse things, and *makrothumia,* which refers to patience toward antagonistic persons.[3] While we can understand this difference and will encounter both in our journey of following Christ, at times these words are used together. One example is when the Apostle Paul describes God's attitude and actions toward us: "Do you think lightly of the riches of His kindness and tolerance and patience, not knowing that the kindness of God leads you to repentance?" (Romans 2:4) Note that not two but three words are used to describe God's character: *kindness, tolerance, and patience.* I, for one, am thankful for all three; together they paint an appealing picture, reminding us that our relational calling toward one another is to pass along what we have so graciously received from God.

While the primary Greek word, *bearing,* is found 15 times in the New Testament, it is most prominently highlighted in two of the paramount relational passages in the New Testament: Ephesians 4 and Colossians 3.

The passage in Ephesians is Paul's transition into the last half of his letter to the church. For three chapters he describes in rich detail *the believer's wealth in Christ;* in the last three chapters he transitions into *the believer's walk.* It is in this application section of Ephesians that he addresses the truth of *bearing with one another.*

143

"I implore you to walk in a manner worthy of the calling with which you have been called, with all humility and gentleness, *with patience, bearing with one another in love*, being diligent to preserve the unity of the Spirit in the bonds of peace" (Ephesians 4:1-3; italics mine).

Paul's point cannot be missed; the primary way we live out our faith, applying the rich doctrinal realities which are ours in Christ, is to walk in a manner worthy of our high calling; we do this in how we relate to one another within the church.

We see this identical truth in Colossians: "As those who have been chosen by God, holy and beloved, put on a heart of compassion, kindness, humility, gentleness, and patience, *bearing with one another*, and forgiving each other, whoever has a complaint against anyone; just as the Lord forgave you, so also should you. Beyond all these things, put on love which is the perfect bond of unity" (Colossians 3:12-14; italics mine).

In comparing this instructive relational passage with the one in Ephesians, there is an obvious similarity; both stress unity, both emphasize essentially the same character qualities (including bearing with one another), and both have as the basis of their appeal God's gracious choice of us. Stated simply, our motivation for keeping our relationships healthy is God's sovereign grace in bringing us into His family, the one that will be ours for eternity.

As mentioned earlier, the word translated *bear or bearing* is found 15 times in the New Testament. It means *to show tolerance, patience, or forbearance, to put up with, or to endure.*[4] Even so, it is important to understand that the Apostle Paul is not instructing us to overlook immoral living or tolerate heretical teaching, for he renounced both. In other New Testament passages, we are taught how to deal with problems of this nature. But in these passages Paul's appeal is for us to patiently bear with one another's weaknesses and idiosyncrasies, recognizing each person as unique, and at different levels of spiritual maturity.

144

A common testing time we all experience is when someone's opinion is different from ours, even if our disagreement is relatively minor, having nothing to do with the non-negotiables of our faith. A well-known saying in the church for several centuries was this: *"In essentials, unity; in nonessentials, liberty; in all things, charity."* Though often attributed to one of the well-known theologians such as Augustine, the statement comes from an otherwise undistinguished German theologian of the early seventeenth century, Rupertus Meldenius.[5] Philip Schaff, the eminent nineteenth-century church historian referred to this wise saying as "the watchword for Christian peacemakers."[6] Inherent in this enlightening statement is the recognition that those who are truly committed to peace are also deeply committed to *bear with one another in love,* giving liberty in the non-essential matters. In paraphrasing this saying, I sometimes commented to our church in Indiana that *we seek to major on the majors, and minor on the minors, and have the wisdom to know the difference.* Bearing with one another is certainly *a major* for healthy church relationships.

In an earlier chapter, I stated that the one another's provide a summation or synopsis of our Lord's relational design for His church, namely, that we love one another as He has loved us. While my approach is for us to examine several of the one another's one chapter at a time, or sermon by sermon, having found this to be valuable for me, it is not my intent to separate them. What we see in the Epistles is a constant intersecting and overlapping as the writer explains how they are to be applied in the life of the church. An example of this is our one another for this chapter.

Bearing with one another is closely related to at least three other commands I write about in this book: accept one another, let us not judge one another, and forgive one another. It would be almost impossible to obey one of these without the others coming into play. Let me explain.

145

Paul admonished the church in Rome to "accept one another, just as Christ also accepted us to the glory of God" (Romans 15:7). His succinct appeal is the conclusion to the issue he introduced earlier in the first verse of Romans 14: "Now accept the one who is weak in faith, but not for the purpose of passing judgment on his opinions" (Romans 14:1). As explained in an earlier chapter, believers in the church at Rome were at odds with one another over non-essential matters such as the observance of special days and diets. In dealing with this Paul explained, "Each person must be fully convinced in his own mind" (Romans 14:5). He went on to state, "Therefore, let us not judge one another anymore" (Romans 14:13). By including the word *anymore*, judging was occurring, meaning that in working through these issues, those who were hurt would need to forgive, based on the pardon they had already received from the Lord. In moving to his conclusion, Paul then writes, "Now we who are strong ought to *bear* the weaknesses of those without strength and not just please ourselves" (Romans 15:1; italics mine).

While the circumstances and issues vary from one church to another, *accepting, not judging, forgiving, and bearing with one another*, are linked hand to hand, and all are expressions of Christlike love. Instead of rejecting, we are to accept; instead of being critical judges, we are to stop judging; instead of holding a grudge and becoming bitter and resentful, we are to be quick to forgive; and in place of an intolerant attitude, we are to patiently bear with one another in love.

This again brings us face to face with the truth that this one another, like all the others, is reciprocal and mutual; there is a commonality because of our shared relationship with Jesus Christ. When Linda and I were married, the vows we exchanged were not, *"I will bear with you as long as you will bear with me, but if you stop bearing with me, I will no longer bear with you."* No, our vows were not conditional as they often are in so many marriages and families today; they were unconditional. My commitment was to love and honor her for better or for worse, for richer or for poorer, in sickness and in health; to love and to cherish till death causes us to part. She made identical commitments to me; this is what is meant by exchanging vows. They were not contingent on whether the other person followed through or not. Reciprocation is nice and how it is meant to be in marriage, in families, and the church; but each one of us must give our response to God's command, and our final accountability will be to Him.

While relationships in the church are not at the same level of intimacy as in marriage, we are linked in a much deeper way than most of us comprehend, and this connection is by God's design. "We who are many, are one body in Christ, and individually members one of another" (Romans 12:5). In contrast to marriage, which is for this life only, our spiritual connection as brothers and sisters in Christ is for eternity.

Some years ago, Bill and Gloria Gaither wrote a song entitled, *Getting Used to the Family of God.* The lyrics include these words, "Going together, enjoying the trip; getting used to the family I'll spend eternity with."[7] Yes, if we do not learn to bear with one another in this life, we will certainly learn how to do it in eternity. This is one of the reasons I often use the phrase, *God's forever family*, for this is who He made us to be.

When we begin to embrace this Biblical truth of our eternal calling, there will be an increased sense of urgency in *walking worthy of the calling with which we have been called.* As we earlier observed, a major part of this is *bearing with one another in love,* not as an end in and of itself, but for the purpose of preserving the unity of the Spirit in the bond of peace (Ephesians 4:1-3). Having this commitment to the health and unity of the church is one of the attitudes that identifies us as true followers of Jesus Christ. If we are intolerant with others, impatient in our dealings with our brothers and sisters in Christ, then we are not walking in a manner worthy of our high calling in Christ, nor are we being diligent to preserve the unity of the Spirit in the bonds of peace.

The relational emphasis so prominent in Colossians 3 and Ephesians 4 has its origin in Jesus' high priestly prayer in John 17, prayed only hours before the cross. In that prayer, as we saw in an earlier chapter, Jesus prayed for the unity of His immediate followers, but also for all those who would believe on Him through their word. His prayer was for the church to experience the same unity Jesus and His Father enjoyed. Some years ago as I was studying and meditating on Jesus' request for unity, a thought I had never had before came into my mind: *Jesus answers my prayers – If I will be diligent in seeking to preserve the unity of the Spirit in the bonds of peace, I can be part of answering His prayer!* I make this comment recognizing His prayer for unity has already been answered, for His church is one! For this reason, Paul instructs us not to work toward unity, but *to preserve or maintain* the unity of the Spirit already established in the bonds of peace.

Unity in the church is a passion God placed in my heart many years ago. In reflecting on its origin, I believe it began with a lesson I learned in our marriage. Like most people I did not enjoy conflict, and when it surfaced in the early years of our marriage, I tended to run, doing everything I could to avoid it. But as God worked through His word to reveal His beautiful plan for marriage, I discovered something I disliked even more passionately than conflict, and that was *unresolved conflict.* As a result, my motivation was to do anything I could to see the conflict resolved so that we might again have peace. This is what we have pursued in our marriage and throughout our family, and it has been and continues to be my passion in the church.

While bearing with one another might appear to some as one of the least important of the one another's, I cannot view it that way at all. Again, I return to the example we see in Jesus perfectly bearing with His often immature disciples, each one with difficult issues. The bottom line, as it is in almost every chapter, is to look to Jesus as our example, trusting Him to progressively reproduce His character in us. It is also helpful for each of us to remember that "love bears all things" (I Corinthians 13:7).

Chapter Twelve Discussion Questions

1. Have you been able to identify habits or practices in your life where you need forbearing grace from others? Could you share one of them?
2. What have you learned about patiently bearing with your spouse or members of your family? How can we determine when it is time to discuss some difficult marriage or family issues and not simply bear with them?
3. Read again Paul's testimony in I Timothy 1:13-15 and discuss how this enabled him to be more patient and forbearing with others.
4. Talk through the importance of the saying mentioned in this chapter: "In essentials, unity; in non-essentials, liberty; in all things, charity." In earlier years, the word charity was commonly used to describe agape love.
5. Give an example where you have seen multiple one another's coming into play in your relationships or others you have observed.
6. Share a memorable example of someone you have observed who demonstrated an abundant amount of patience and forbearance such as the lady the author mentioned who patiently cared for her mother under trying circumstances.

Chapter Thirteen
Submit to One Another

"Submit to one another out of reverence for Christ."

Ephesians 5:21[1]

What is the first thought that comes to your mind when you read the *one another* verse for this chapter? Whatever it is, we can agree that submission is not a popular topic in today's culture. The thought of submission is totally opposed to how the world operates and goes against fallen human nature as well. Like the citizens in Jesus' parable who hated the man their master put over them while he was away on a journey, the attitude of most is: "We do not want this man to reign over us" (Luke 19:14).

When we turn to the church, sadly, the attitude is often not that different. Even though submission is prominent in the teaching of the New Testament, Christians find it difficult to be subject to one another, and in other areas where Scripture teaches that we are to submit.

Wives, as most married men are aware, are instructed to submit to their husbands. We see this admonition three times in the writings of Paul (Ephesians 5:22; Colossians 3:18; and Titus 2:5), and once in Peter's first epistle (I Peter 3:1). Children also are to obey and submit to their parents, showing them honor as well (Ephesians 6:1-2; Colossians 3:20). In this same context, with slavery being pervasive in the Roman Empire, slaves were instructed, "Be obedient to those who are your masters according to the flesh" (Ephesians 6:4). While today's culture is vastly different, this principle carries over into the relationship between employers and employees.

Christians are also directed to submit to civil authorities: "Every person is to be subject to the governing authorities. For there is no authority except from God, and those which exist are established by God" (Romans 13:1). We see this in the Apostle Peter's writings as well: "Submit yourself for the Lord's sake to every human institution, whether to a king as the one in authority, or to governors sent by him for the punishment of evildoers and the praise of those who do right" (I Peter 2:13-14).

This truth is being severely tested even as I write, as our nation continues to struggle with the COVID-19 pandemic. Churches ceased all public gatherings in the beginning because they saw this as their clear biblical responsibility. As time passed, however, this resolve is being tested as the pandemic is not nearly as extensive as first projected. Many church leaders now sense that some in government may be guilty of a constitutional overreach, denying Christians our God-given, first amendment right to gather for worship. If this is the case, we wonder when we will reach the same decision as the apostles in the first-century church when they declared, "We must obey God rather than men" (Acts 5:29). There is currently an escalating tension between governmental authority, ecclesiastical responsibility, and our constitutional rights as Americans, and to such an extent as we have not witnessed in our country. Only time will tell how long this will continue, and how the church will respond.

Scripture also instructs Christians to submit to their leaders in the church: "Obey your leaders and submit to them, for they keep watch over your souls, as those who must give an account" (Hebrews 13:17). But the Bible also instructs elders not to "lord it over those allotted to your charge, but proving to be examples to the flock" (I Peter 5:3). To be a spiritual leader in a local church is a solemn responsibility, and all who accept it must do it as unto the Lord.

Above all, we are to submit to God, who is the sovereign authority over the entire universe: "God is opposed to the proud, but gives grace to the humble. *Submit yourselves, therefore, to God*" (James 4:7; italics mine). Our ultimate submission and allegiance must be to Him alone.

What is beyond dispute is that submission is taught in the New Testament, and is to be part of the lifestyle of every Christian. Gene Getz explains, "Submission is a synonym for obedience. In its most general use, it means to yield to another person's admonition or advice. In Scripture, it appears in contexts describing servanthood, humility, respect, reverence, honor, being teachable, and openness. All these are for one basic purpose – obedience to Jesus Christ."[1]

Our focus in this chapter is about submission between Christians, what it means to submit to one another out of reverence for Christ. Of the 58 one another's in the New Testament, this is often the most difficult for Christians to discuss, and even more demanding to apply. Again, Gene Getz provides this helpful insight: "Mutual submission, even by those who are in authority, is a distinctive concept made possible by Jesus Christ. When Christ came into this world, He brought into being a whole new approach to functional relationships between people. In the 'Gentile world,' as Jesus called it, there is no such thing as mutual submission. The fallen man operates out of selfish motives. He has little or no interest in helping others reach their goals – except when it might benefit himself. He may listen to someone else's advice, but usually not out of respect and honor."[2]

As we narrow our focus, the next step is to examine the context where our key verse is found. The first truth we see is that to submit to one another in our own strength is an impossible task. What we learn from Paul's instruction is that submission is the overflow of an indispensable spiritual reality, one that is God's will for every believer.

In looking at the context more carefully, we see that submitting to one another is the byproduct of the Spirit-filled life. There is a grammatical connection between Ephesians 5:21, where submission is stated, and Ephesians 5:18 where Paul's directive is given about being filled with the Spirit; it is all one sentence. If we are controlling our own lives and being dominated by our flesh, we have neither the desire nor the power to submit. But when we submit to the Spirit who resides within us, He enables us to relate to one another with a submissive attitude, out of our mutual reverence for Christ.

Because there is often confusion about the ministry of the Holy Spirit, I want to seek to provide some clarification before explaining how these crucial truths are linked to submitting to one another. *First, being filled with the Holy Spirit is God's will for every believer.* "So then, do not be foolish, but understand what the will of the Lord is. And do not get drunk with wine, for that is dissipation, but be filled with the Spirit" (Ephesians 5:17-18). To be filled with wine to the point of dissipation, or overindulgence, is to be out of control. In contrast, to be filled with the Spirit is to be under His control. Let me clarify by explaining what being filled with the Spirit does not mean.

- *It does not mean that we receive the Holy Spirit.* This is because the Holy Spirit came to indwell us the moment we trusted in Christ and were saved. The New Testament often speaks of the bodies of Christians being the *temple of the Holy Spirit.* The Apostle Paul explains, "If anyone does not have the Spirit of Christ, he does not belong to Him" (Romans 8:9). From the moment we are born again and made alive in Christ, the Holy Spirit comes to live within us.

- *It does not mean we are baptized with the Holy Spirit, for this also took place the moment of our salvation when we first trusted Christ.* Again, the Apostle Paul also makes this clear: "For by one Spirit we were all baptized into one body, whether Jews or Greeks, slaves or free men, and we were all made to drink of one Spirit" (I Corinthians 12:13). Note that he does not say "some" but "all" were baptized by One Spirit.

- *It does not mean being sealed with the Spirit, for this also took place when we first believed.* Here again are the words of the Apostle Paul: "In Him, you also, after listening to the message of the truth, the gospel of your salvation – having also believed, you were sealed in Him with the Holy Spirit of promise" (Ephesians 1:13).

From these three truths, we can settle an issue that many Christians fail to understand. Not one time in the New Testament are we ever commanded to be indwelt by the Holy Spirit; not once are we ever commanded to be baptized by the Holy Spirit, and there is never a place where we are commanded to be sealed by the Holy Spirit. Each one of these precious realities took place when we responded to God's gracious call and were saved and became a member of God's family.

In contrast, however, as we see in Ephesians 5:17-18, we are commanded to be filled with the Holy Spirit; this is unquestionably God's will for us. To be filled and controlled by the Holy Spirit is not optional for Christians; it is a mandate.

In his helpful commentary on Ephesians, John MacArthur writes. "Although every Christian is indwelt, baptized, and sealed with the Holy Spirit, unless he is also filled with the Holy Spirit he will live in spiritual weakness, retardation, frustration, and defeat."[3] Sadly, many Christians never experience the reality of the filling of the Spirit, settling for a prolonged period of spiritual infancy, failing to grow to Christian maturity. The writer of Hebrews describes this distressing condition, "By this time you should be teachers of the Word, but you need someone to teach you again the elementary principles of the Word; you have come to need milk and not solid food" (Hebrews 5:12).

But now we turn to the second point: *being filled with the Holy Spirit involves moment by moment submission to the Holy Spirit's control.* "The verb is in the present tense – 'keep on being filled'- so it is a reality we are meant to enjoy constantly, not simply on special occasions. And the verb is passive, meaning we do not fill ourselves but trust the Holy Spirit to fill us."[4] This wonderful reality is meant to be an ongoing, moment by moment, relational submission to the Holy Spirit's control. When we sin, it is important that we keep short accounts with God and quickly confess our sins, being assured of His ongoing, faithful forgiveness, resubmitting ourselves to the Holy Spirit's control.

Paul makes a related point in his letter to the Galatians, namely, that being filled and walking in the power of the Spirit is a learning process. "Since we have been made alive by the Spirit, let us also walk by the Spirit" (Galatians 5:25). This word for *walk* is also used to describe a child *learning to walk*. This is an accurate picture of being continuously filled with the Spirit, for it is a learning process. The New International Version captures it well, "Keep in step with the Spirit"[5] (Galatians 5:25 NIV). Our Christian life begins with a miraculous spiritual birth, and the Holy Spirit seals us as belonging to God, taking up His residence in us. Though He will never leave or forsake us, He can be *grieved* (See Ephesians 4:30) when we become self-centered and fail to yield the control of our lives to Him.

Sometimes I illustrate this truth by talking about our marriage. The mark of a healthy marriage is not the love and devotion Linda and I have shared in the past, as meaningful and lovely as that was; nor is it the faithful commitment we anticipate in the future. The health of our marriage is the relationship we have with one another in the present, and this means keeping our relationship current with nothing blocking it. This is how it is in our relationship with the Holy Spirit; we want Him to have day by day, moment by moment control. This is God's will for our lives, as we have seen.

Thirdly, being filled with the Holy Spirit is how God designed for His work to be accomplished. An enlightening Old Testament summary of this is found in the book of Zachariah, at a time when the people had returned to Jerusalem and were rebuilding the temple after having spent 70 years of captivity in Babylon. God sent these words to Zerubbabel, the governor of Judah, to encourage him as to how the task would be completed: "Not by might, nor by power, but by My Spirit', says the Lord" (Zachariah 4:6). Time and time again I have returned to this truth in my life and ministry as I have waited on Him in faith to do His work.

The word for *fill* in the Greek is *pleroo*, and three helpful word pictures are associated with it. "It means more than filling something up, as when someone pours water in a glass up to the rim. It was used in three additional senses that give insight into Paul's meaning. First, it was often used of the wind filling a sail and thereby carrying the ship along. Second, it carries the idea of permeation and was used for salt's saturating meat to flavor and preserve it. Third, *pleroo* has the connotation of total control."[5] Each picture uniquely reveals the absolute necessity of the Holy Spirit's power and control in our lives. Whatever work He has for us, including submitting to one another out of reverence for Christ, this can only be done as He provides the power.

Those who have carefully studied the life of Christ understand that His entire life and ministry was carried out in the power of the Holy Spirit. "Jesus, full of the Holy Spirit, returned from the Jordan and was led around by the Spirit in the wilderness" (Luke 4:1). After forty days of being tempted by the devil, we read, "And Jesus returned to Galilee in the power of the Spirit" (Luke 4:14). Soon after Jesus' temptation, He went into the synagogue in Nazareth, where He had been brought up, and read from Isaiah 61, a passage every Jew understood as referring to the Messiah: "The Spirit of the Lord is upon Me…" (Luke 4:18). When He had finished, with the eyes of everyone in the synagogue fixed on Him, Jesus closed the scroll and declared, "Today this Scripture has been fulfilled in your hearing" (Luke 4:21). From the New Testament, we know that Jesus is not only our Savior and Lord; He is our example, and He lived His entire life under the control of the Holy Spirit.

One additional word picture I heard many years ago of this truth has been especially helpful. "The Christian who is filled with the Holy Spirit can be compared to a glove. Until the glove is filled by a hand, a glove is powerless and useless. It is designed to do work, but it can do no work by itself. It works only when the hand controls and uses it. The glove's only work is the hand's work. A Christian can accomplish no more without being filled with the Holy Spirit than a glove can accomplish without being filled with a hand."[6]

Fourthly, being filled with the Holy Spirit produces distinct results, one being - submitting to one another out of reverence for Christ. Even though I have given you this somewhat detailed explanation before returning to our *one another* focus for this chapter, my desire is that you understand the indispensable link between the Spirit filling and controlling our lives, and the issue of submission.

The truth emerging from Paul's enlightening paragraph is that submitting is the last of a series of participles describing the overflow of being filled and controlled by the Holy Spirit. Here again, is the passage: "Be filled with the Spirit, *speaking* to one another in psalms, hymns, and spiritual songs, *singing* and *making melody* in your hearts to the Lord, always *giving thanks* for all things in the name of our Lord Jesus Christ to God, even the Father, *being subject* to one another out of reverence for Christ" (Ephesians 5:18-21; italics mine). Grammatically speaking, while *submitting to one another* is not an actual command, some versions translate it as such. The Greek language does permit imperative participles, though some Greek students refer to them as grammatical anomalies. What is clear, however, is that biblical submission will only become part of our lives as we yield to the power of the Spirit who lives within us.

One of the most interesting features of Ephesians 5:21, where we read of being subject or submitting to one another, is how the Apostle Paul uses it as a topic sentence to transition into his practical teaching on Christian marriage, and then to his instruction to parents and children, and masters and slaves. He begins in this way: "Wives, be subject to your own husbands, as to the Lord. For the husband is head of the wife, as Christ also is the head of the church, He Himself being the Savior of the body. But as the church is subject to Christ, so the wives also ought to be to their husbands in everything" (Ephesians 5:22-24).

As we bring this chapter to a close, I want to set forth three applications linked to the enlightening phrase which concludes verse 21 – *out of reverence for Christ.* Highly respected British pastor of an earlier generation, Dr. Martin Lloyd Jones, refers to this lovely expression as "the motive that governs the whole of Christian living."[7] Seeing it this way means that our supreme passion as we relate to one another is meant to be our reverence for Christ. If Christians could conscientiously follow this truth, it would completely transform our relationships, but it must be put into practice. So, what does this mean?

First, having a reverence for Christ reminds us that He is present in all our relationships. A James Lawrence wall hanging often found in Christian homes succinctly captures this truth: "Christ is the Head of this home, the unseen Guest at every meal, the Silent Listener to every conversation."[8] Our Lord desires to be acknowledged in our homes, not merely as a Guest, but as our beloved Host. Even though He is *unseen* and *silent* does not make Him any less present.

If we are thinking biblically, we know our Lord is always present when Christians gather. This is because the Holy Spirit, the Spirit of Christ (Romans 8:9), lives within each Christian. Jesus often assured His followers of this truth: "Where two or three are gathered together in My name, there I am in the midst" (Matthew 18:20). "I am with you always, even to the end of the age" (Matthew 28:20). "I will never desert you, nor will I ever forsake you" (Hebrews 13:5). Recognizing and affirming His presence is the essential first step toward showing our reverence for Christ.

Second, having a reverence for Christ keeps our attitudes and words from going into a downward spiral in how we relate to one another. We are all too familiar with what can happen if our lives are not submitted to the Holy Spirit. When we fail to have reverence for our ever-present Lord, our attitude, actions, and words can quickly deteriorate into a downward spiral. The consequence is that we deeply wound our brother and sister in Christ, grieving the Holy Spirit as well (Ephesians 4:30).

Third, having a reverence for Christ enables us to maintain a teachable spirit to receive whatever truth He intends to bring to us through others. The overarching truth of the *one another* admonitions is that God's plan for bringing each one of us to spiritual maturity is to use our brothers and sisters in Christ; He plans to use us in their lives as well. A reverence for Christ assures us that we will value each member of His body, whether that person be a new believer, or one who is our most severe critic. Submission to one another is only possible as we are completely submitted to Christ.

May the Spirit of Christ give us a reverence for Him each time we gather with our fellow believers, and may we know in experience what it means to be submissive to one another with Him foremost in our minds.

Chapter Thirteen Discussion Questions

1. Why does submission tend to be difficult for most people?
2. With submission being the result of the Holy Spirit controlling our lives, what are some of His ministries described in this chapter? Describe how one or more of these truths are encouraging to you in your Christian life.
3. Walking in the Spirit is a learning process, much like a child learning to walk. What have you discovered that has accelerated learning in your walk with Christ?
4. Four word pictures are given as to what it means to be filled with the Holy Spirit. Which of these is most helpful as you think of His work in and through you?
5. Martin Lloyd Jones refers to the phrase at the end of Ephesians 5:21 – "out of reference for Christ" as *the motive that governs the whole of Christian living.* What are some practical things we can do to make this a reality in our relationships?
6. What is one application truth you hope to take away from this chapter?

Chapter Fourteen
Encourage One Another

"Therefore, encourage one another and build up one another, just as you are also doing."

I Thessalonians 5:11

Our relational admonition for this chapter is one of the most prominent in the New Testament, second only to *love one another.* Knowing His children in all generations would be susceptible to discouragement, God saw to it that the command to *encourage one another* would be oft-repeated in his Word.

In the early 1980s, I was invited to speak for a week in a beautiful country church in the corn and soybean farmlands of Southern Indiana. My wife and I first became acquainted with the church in the 1960s, and the people had asked me to preach there on other occasions over the years. Their pastor at the time of this visit was a delightful young man who had grown up on a farm in Kentucky before sensing God calling him to preach.

During our week there, the church followed the pattern of our previous visits, scheduling lunch and dinner for us in the homes of families in the church, most of whom we already knew because of our history with the congregation. Wherever we went that week, the people gave glowing reports about their pastor and his wife, sharing examples of what they appreciated. They told of how he helped the farmers with their plowing in the spring and was back again in the fall to assist with the harvest. The report was that he did this not only for those in the church but for everyone in the community. We heard about how he helped widows and elderly people with needed repairs around their property. They told of how he and his wife would take the vegetables from their garden and make them available at a roadside stand in front of their home with a sign that read, *Free Vegetables – Help Yourself!* The parishioners were also complimentary of his preaching, and how faithful he was to visit them when they were sick, at the hospital for surgery, or had some other emergency. From everything I could see, he was the perfect fit for this rural, farming community.

Once our week was complete, we returned to our home and ministry in Tyler, Texas. Some months later, while talking by phone to this young pastor's father-in-law, the news was that in *discouragement* the pastor had resigned from his position, returning to farming in Kentucky. I mentioned how surprised I was, especially after having heard such affirming words from almost everyone in his congregation. His father-in-law responded by saying, "Tom, the people told me some of those things as well, but they apparently never told him. In his heart he felt he was not doing a good job, and in his discouragement went back to farming."

That disheartening experience enabled me to see more clearly than ever before that everyone needs encouragement, even pastors. I should say - *especially pastors* - as I have spoken to several over the years who became discouraged to the point of walking away from the ministry, as appeared to be the case with the young man whose story I just related. The rest of the story for him, however, is good news; he did return to farming in Kentucky, but to preaching as well where he had a fruitful ministry spanning several years.

Missionaries also often require encouragement. My father-in-law, William A. Gillam, a highly respected missionary statesman, experienced deep discouragement following his first four-year term of service in Colombia, so much so that he knew it would be

163

impossible for him to return unless God brought renewed strength and encouragement. Thankfully, God worked in unique ways to give him the reassurance he so desperately needed. He was strengthened to return to Medellin, Colombia, where he served with distinction in a fruitful ministry spanning the 1940s and into the mid-1950s, before moving into a broader ministry in missions.

There have certainly been times in my life and ministry where I too became discouraged, questioning if I could continue, but each time God faithfully brought the needed encouragement. One of God's greatest gifts to me is my wife, one of the most faithful encouragers I have ever known. Without her prayer, reassurance, and affirming words, I could not have persevered for these years. God has also been gracious to prompt His people in our church to write notes of encouragement, letters of appreciation, or provide other loving gestures at appropriate times to lift my spirits and keep my heart encouraged.

Some years ago I read these inspiring words from William Barclay: "One of the highest human duties is the duty of encouragement...it is easy to laugh at men's ideals; it is very easy to pour cold water on their enthusiasm; it is easy to discourage others. The world is full of discouragers. We have a Christian duty to encourage one another. Many a time a word of thanks or appreciation or cheer has kept a man on his feet. Blessed is the man who speaks such a word."[1]

Because of the richness of the Greek language, *to encourage* is a phrase with multiple usages, and the meaning cannot be fully captured with one word. Because of this, we see the translators exercising freedom to use the word that best fits the biblical context.

The noun form of the word is *paraclete*, and is the term Jesus used with His disciples to refer to the Holy Spirit: "I will ask the Father, and He will give you another *Helper* (*Paraclete*), that He may be with you forever" (John 14:16). William Barclay offers this helpful insight: "The word *paraclete* means someone who is called in; but it is the reason why the person is called in that gives the word its distinctive associations. The Greeks used the word in a variety of ways. A *paraclete* might be a person called in to give witness in a law court in someone's favor; he might be an advocate called in to plead someone's cause when a person was under a charge which would issue into serious penalty; he might be an expert called in to advise in some difficult situation. He might be called in, for example, when a company of soldiers was depressed and dispirited, to put new courage into their minds and hearts. Always a *paraclete* is someone called in to help when the person who calls him is in trouble or distress or doubt or bewilderment."[2] The complexity of the circumstances is why we see paraclete being variously translated – Helper, Enabler, or Encourager.

The verb form of the word is *parakaleo,* meaning to call or come alongside. While situations vary, the person coming alongside is there to assist in whatever way is necessary, with the result being that the person receives the needed assistance and encouragement. Gene Getz provides this explanation: "The basic Greek word, *parakaleo,* appears in several forms in the New Testament. At times, the word is translated "to exhort, to admonish or to teach'; at other times 'to beg, entreat, or beseech.' It is also translated 'to console; to encourage; to comfort.' But the basic word is always used for one primary purpose – to describe actions that enable Christians to be built up in Christ, or help them to build up one another in Christ."[3]

We often speak today of being able to cope with things. As we saw from Jesus' use of the word *paraclete*, this is precisely the work of the Holy Spirit. Jesus explained that while He was with His disciples, the time would soon come following His departure when the Spirit would indwell them, even as He does with all who come to Christ in faith. The word Jesus used, translated Helper in the NASB, literally means - *another just like Me!* Even as Jesus lived among His apostles as their Helper/Encourager for three years, after His

165

departure the Holy Spirit would be their foremost encourager, and so He is for us. The truth we are highlighting in this chapter, however, is that God plans to also use believers, empowered by the Spirit who resides within them, to be a source of encouragement to one another.

Before we examine other New Testament passages for application, let me share a favorite of mine from the Old Testament character of Job. When his three friends arrived to comfort him, in seeing his deep pain, they could do nothing more than sit down and weep, saying absolutely nothing to him for seven days and seven nights. (See Job 2:11-13.) The first friend who ventured to speak was Eliphaz. Included in his words was a reminder of how Job had been an encourager to others: "Behold, you have instructed many, and you have strengthened the weak; your words have kept men on their feet" (Job 4:3-4 Moffatt)[4]. I love that phrase! Speaking a word of encouragement at the opportune time can indeed *keep men (and women) on their feet*. Oh, that we might learn to speak such words! This is surely one of the applications of what the writer of Proverbs had in mind when he wrote, "Like apples of gold in settings of silver is a word spoken in right circumstances" (Proverbs 25:11).

With this background, I want to present some New Testament truths to help us as we seek to *encourage one another*. *First, encouragement has biblical truth as its source.* Those of us who are seasoned believers know that nothing brings encouragement in our sorrow and distress like the Word of God. When the Apostle Paul was nearing the end of his epistle to the church at Rome, he beautifully highlighted this point: "For whatever was written in earlier times was written for our instruction, that through perseverance and *the encouragement of the Scriptures* we might have hope" (Romans 15:4; italics mine). What a wonderful phrase – *the encouragement of the Scriptures!*

On countless occasions, times when I felt spiritually dry, defeated, and discouraged, and at other seasons when I was bewildered and confused, God used His Word to bring spiritual encouragement. It often came through my daily quiet time of reading the Scripture, and at other times through my wife or another friend with whom I was meeting. Sometimes it was through a sermon or while listening to a recorded message. At other times God encouraged me while listening to the great hymns of the faith which are abounding with God's Word. In each case, the source was the same - *the encouragement of the Scriptures.* His Word has often been like fresh water to my thirsty soul, good news from a distant land, or as "a lamp to my feet and a light to my path" (Psalm 119:105).

God has given me high honor and solemn responsibility as a pastor to communicate His Word week after week, month after month, year after year, dating back to when I was in college. The heart of my calling, as I now see it, is identical to the one given to Timothy by the Apostle Paul: "Be diligent to present yourself approved to God as a workman who does not need to be ashamed, accurately handling the word of truth" (II Timothy 2:15). The fruit of my study is being able to bring *the encouragement of the Scriptures* to those who are hurting. In the flyleaf of my little New Testament is a definition of preaching I heard several years ago: *"Preaching is communicating the revelation of God into human situations where men and women sin, and hate, and fear, and weep, and lose heart."* Though I do not recall the source, it reminds me that it is God's Word I am called to communicate to a troubled, needy world, and it is His Word He has promised to bless.

Second, encouragement brings protection against sin's deceitfulness. The Epistle to the Hebrews contains several warnings, along with many incredible promises; this is one of the solemn warnings: "Encourage *one another* day after day, as long as it is still called 'Today,' so that none of you will be hardened by the deceitfulness of sin" (Hebrews 3:13).

Christians have long identified three fronts on which believers can expect to be attacked: the world, the flesh, and the devil. The writer of Hebrews simply warns against *the deceitfulness of sin,* without identifying its source. His answer, given for our protection, is for us to be so connected to other believers, *encouraging one another day after day,* that we avoid becoming ensnared by sin's deceitfulness. In his book, *The Fight,* John White states, "It need not surprise us that as an image to convey the nature of Christian living, the Holy Spirit uses that of warfare. War is not something that illustrates aspects of Christian living. *Christian living is war.*"[5]

Whatever our background, each one of us will be tempted at some point to question if Jesus is enough, and this is where we need one another's encouragement. This was particularly true of those being addressed by the writer of Hebrews; they were devout Jews who had turned to Christ. The MacArthur Study Bible captures well the context of Hebrews 3:13: "Both individual accountability and corporate responsibility are intended in this admonition. As long as the distressing days were upon them and they were tempted to return to the ineffective Levitical system, they were to encourage one another to identify completely with Jesus Christ."[6] This reminder ought to always be at the heart of the encouragement we give to one another. Paul reminded the churches of Colossae: "In Him you have been made complete" (Colossians 2:10). Nothing more needs to be added to our salvation; Jesus is enough!

Third, the goal of encouragement is to build others up in their faith. We see this in the church of Thessalonica, one of the most dynamic in the New Testament. In his first letter to them, the Apostle Paul gave this instruction: "Therefore, encourage and build up one another, just as you also are doing" (I Thessalonians 5:11).

Note that Paul was simply urging them to persevere in what was already their common practice, namely, encouraging and building up one another. Oh, that this would be the practice in every church!

An exemplary New Testament example of encouragement is Joseph, the Levite. We know him best as Barnabas, the nickname given to him by the Apostles, meaning *Son of Encouragement*. (See Acts 4:36.) Each time we see Barnabas in the book of Acts, his heart of encouragement is shining forth. His generosity encouraged the infant but rapidly growing church in Jerusalem, enabling them to have the financial means to meet the needs of the people (Acts 4:32-37). When Saul of Tarsus was a suspicious new convert, seeking to associate with the disciples in Jerusalem, none of whom were believing in him, it was the encourager, Barnabas, who courageously enabled Saul to connect with the church (Acts 9:26-28). When the Gospel was spreading to the Gentiles, and large numbers believed in the city of Antioch, it was kindhearted Barnabas who was sent to encourage them (Acts 11:19-24). Understanding it was God's plan to reach the Gentile world, Barnabas searched for Saul and recruited him to join him in Antioch, where they taught considerable numbers (Acts 11:25-26). In the providence of God, the church in Antioch, not Jerusalem, became the missionary-sending church in the New Testament, with Barnabas and Saul (Paul) being the first ones sent forth (Acts 13:1-5). And it was Barnabas who continued to believe in God's faithful work in John Mark, despite his earlier failures, even when Paul refused to believe in him (Acts 15:36-40). Through the encouragement of Barnabas, John Mark was able to recover and go on to have a fruitful ministry, including authoring one of the four Gospels. If you want an example of how to be an encourager in the church, look no further than Barnabas. A good start would be to prayerfully read the various references I included in my description of him.

Fourth, encouragement has grace at the heart of its message. This point can easily be made from God's Word, but I make it from my personal experience as well. While the word *gospel* means good news, the liberating message of grace is at the heart of it. In his letter to the churches of Colossae, the Apostle Paul explained how "the word of truth, the gospel...has come to you, just as in all the world also it is constantly bearing fruit and increasing, even as it has been doing in you since the first day you heard of it and *understood the grace of God in truth...*" (Colossians 1:5-6; italics mine). The greatest and most lasting encouragement that has ever come to me was when I too *understood the grace of God in truth!*

This means that salvation is neither received nor maintained by human achievement, but only through God's sovereign work of grace, described by Paul in Ephesians: "Blessed be the God and Father of our Lord Jesus Christ, who has blessed us with every spiritual blessing in the heavenly places in Christ, just as He chose us in Him before the foundation of the world..." (Ephesians 1:3-4). Paul goes on to explain that God's sovereign choice from eternity was *"to the praise of the glory of His grace"* (Ephesians 1:6), and *"according to the riches of His grace, which He lavished on us"* (Ephesians 1:7-8), and that it would all be *"to the praise of His glory"* (Ephesians 1:12, 14; italics mine).

If you fail to have grace at the heart of your encouragement, those you are seeking to assist will remain under the guilt of personal obligation, never experiencing and enjoying their freedom in Christ. Hear Paul's words of warning to the Galatians: "I am amazed that you are so quickly deserting Him who called you by the grace of Christ for a different gospel; which is not another, but there are some who are disturbing you and want to distort the gospel of Christ" (Galatians 1:6-7). Later in his letter, Paul explains, "It was for freedom that Christ set us free; therefore, keep standing firm and do not be subject again to a yoke of bondage" (Galatians 5:1). The message of grace alone brings the freedom of which Paul writes.

One additional example of encouragement comes from Paul's second letter to the church of Thessalonica: "Now may our Lord Jesus Christ, and God our Father, who loved us and gave us *eternal encouragement and good hope through grace*, encourage and strengthen your hearts in every good work and word" (II Thessalonians 2:16-17). What a beautiful summary of biblical encouragement, the message I desire to give to others.

Grace is the distinctive word of the Christian faith. There is nothing comparable to it in any of the religions of the world. Nor is grace found in the message of dedicated but deceived cult members who go door to door with their false teaching, knowing nothing of the message of this glorious truth, and having no assurance of salvation.

As to the significance of grace, J. I. Packer comments: "In the New Testament, *grace* is a word of central importance – the keyword, in fact, of Christianity. Grace is what the New Testament is all about. Its God is 'the God of all grace' (I Peter 5:10); its Holy Spirit is 'the Spirit of grace' (Hebrews 10:29); and all the hopes that it sets forth rest upon 'the grace of the Lord Jesus' (Acts 15:11), the Lord who upheld Paul with the assurance, 'My grace is sufficient for you' (II Corinthians 12:9). 'Grace' says John, 'came through Jesus Christ' (John 1:17); and the news about Jesus is accordingly, 'the gospel of the grace of God' (Acts 20:24)."[7]

For mutual encouragement to become a practical reality, being connected to other believers is essential. Spiritual strength does not come if we are isolated, seeking to make it on our own. We only *experience* the church when our lives are intertwined with other members of Christ's church.

Let me illustrate with a lesson from the Giant Sequoias. In October of 2009, Linda and I moved to Porterville, California. One of the blessings of our location is that we can be at the entrance of Sequoia National Park in less than one hour. In the decade since our move, we have been blessed with numerous guests, especially friends from our church in Indianapolis where I pastored for 24 years. Our typical invitation is for families to spend at least two nights with us, and allow me to be their guide to Sequoia on the first full day of their visit, a task for which I am becoming progressively proficient.

One of the truths I love to share is why the Giant Sequoias are so large and strong, and why they live so long - some more than 2,000 years. One of the primary reasons cannot be seen, for the secret is in the roots. "The sequoias have a matting, shallow, and wide-spreading root system. There is no taproot. They only root to 12 to 14 feet deep even at maturity. A mature sequoia's roots can occupy over one acre of earth and contain over 90,000 cubic feet of soil."[8]

The point I go on to make is that what is true of the Giant Sequoias should also mark our lives as Christians. We flourish and stay encouraged when we have strong relational connections, and because our spiritual roots are intertwined with those of our beloved brothers and sisters in Christ. When this is true, we can "encourage one another," even as God's Word instructs us to do.

Chapter Fourteen Discussion Questions

1. What are some practical ways you can encourage your pastor and other ministry leaders in the church, including those who serve in the nursery and work with children and teens?
2. Read again and respond to William Barclay's quote on our duty to encourage others.
3. What part does God's Word have in encouragement? Why is this so significant? (See Romans 15:4-5)
4. Read Hebrews 3:13 and discuss its application to our relational health in the church. According to this verse, why is encouragement so important?
5. Describe a *Barnabas* in your life. How can we follow his example and be an encourager to others?
6. Why is so important to keep grace prominent as we seek to encourage others?
7. Discuss the relational application of the illustration given about the interconnected root system of the Giant Sequoias.

Chapter Fifteen

Pray for One Another

"Therefore, confess your sins to one another, and pray for one another that you may be healed. The effective prayer of a righteous man can accomplish much."

James 5:16

A common expression often heard in the Christian community and even beyond is - *you are in our thoughts and prayers.* While it is an effortless phrase to verbalize, it is much more difficult to follow through, taking time to bring that person and his or her need to our loving Heavenly Father in prayer. My wife and I were troubled about this tendency a few years back and decided to make a change; we purposed to stop and pray the very moment we heard of a need, and we do this regularly today. Our prayers are not long, but they connect us to God and to that person. As Phillip Yancey comments, "When I pray for another person, I am praying for God to open my eyes so I can see that person as God does, and then enter into that stream of love God already directs toward that person. Something happens when I pray for others in this way. Bringing them into God's presence changes my attitude toward them and ultimately affects our relationship."[1]

While there will always be a certain amount of mystery as to how our prayers and God's sovereignty mesh together, one truth is certain from Scripture – *God has sovereignly chosen to work through the prayers of His people.* Being convinced of this and other biblical assurances about the power of prayer, we pray, even as Jesus did when He was here among us.

After the busiest recorded day in Jesus' life and ministry, for example, Mark writes, "And early in the morning, while it was still dark, Jesus got up, left the house, and went out to a secluded place and prayed there" (Mark 1:35). In his gospel Luke records, "Jesus Himself would often slip away into the wilderness and pray" (Luke 5:16). Before the choosing of the twelve, Luke again writes, "It was at this time that He went off to the mountain to pray, and spent the whole night in prayer to God" (Luke 6:12).

Another example of the priority of prayer in Jesus' life came during a difficult conversation with Simon Peter, "Simon, Simon, Satan has demanded permission to sift you like wheat; but I have prayed for you that your faith would not fail; and you, when once you have turned again, strengthen your brothers" (Luke 22:31-32).

Also recorded for our encouragement and edification is Jesus' high priestly prayer, one He prayed the night of His betrayal and arrest. In it, He interceded for His immediate followers but also, as He stated, "for all those also who believe in Me through their word" (John 17:20). Even at this very moment, we know that "He is able also to save forever those who draw near to God through Him, since He always lives to make intercession for them" (Hebrews 7:25).

This mention of Jesus praying brings us back to my fundamental thesis for this book, one I expressed earlier; *the one another commands have as their source the pattern of relating Jesus demonstrated with His initial followers.* In other words, if we want to discover how God intends for us to relate to one another, Jesus is our model and example! In this chapter on prayer, we know that the first-century church prayed for one another because Jesus earlier set the example by faithfully interceding for the men He had chosen.

With the command to *pray for one another* stated so simply, there is a sense in which it could be discussed and applied as it stands. For the fuller meaning, however, the larger context reveals additional truths about prayer, ones that support and enrich James's call for mutually supportive prayer. Here is the passage we will examine in the pages ahead.

"Is anyone among you suffering? Then he must *pray*. Is anyone cheerful? He is to sing praises. Is any among you sick? Then he must call for the elders of the church and they are to *pray* over him, anointing him with oil in the name of the Lord. And the *prayer* offered in faith will restore the one who is sick, and the Lord will raise him up, and if he has committed sins, they will be forgiven him. Therefore, confess your sins to one another and *pray* for one another so that you may be healed. The effective *prayer* of a righteous man can accomplish much. Elijah was a man with a nature like ours, and he *prayed* earnestly that it would not rain, and it did not rain on the earth for three years and six months. Then he *prayed* again, and the sky poured rain and the earth produced its fruit" (James 5:13-18; italics mine).

You likely noted the recurring emphasis on prayer in this paragraph, with forms of the word used seven times. This indicates that James is sharing multiple lessons about the power of prayer, along with various forms it will take in our lives.

The first truth to capture our attention is *the link between personal prayer and spiritual comfort.* A key to interpreting this passage correctly is to understand the unique word James uses for suffering. "It does not refer to physical illness or some debilitating disease, but to the suffering that comes from enduring evil treatment from those who were hostile toward followers of Christ."[2] Writing with the heart of a pastor, James was deeply concerned because those he dearly loved were being abused, badly treated, and in deep suffering.

When James instructs them to pray, it is in the present tense, so the phrase would read, "Is anyone among you suffering? Then *he must keep on praying.*" When life is difficult and we are growing weary in our sufferings, feeling overwhelmed by our circumstances, we too are to pray and persevere in prayer. As we pour out our hearts to our Heavenly Father in intercession, we receive God's comfort, along with the grace to endure whatever form suffering happens to take in our lives.

It is encouraging to know that God is identified in Scripture as the ultimate source of comfort. "Blessed be the God and Father of our Lord Jesus Christ, the Father of mercies, and the *God of all comfort*, who comforts us in all our affliction...just as the sufferings of Christ are ours in abundance, so also is our comfort abundant in Christ" (II Corinthians 1:3-4; italics mine). The good news is that comfort is promised to match our sufferings, and persevering prayer is the link that enables us to connect with the *God of all comfort*.

James continues, "Is anyone cheerful? Let him sing praises" (James 5:13). Cheerful describes those who had remained strong, being able to maintain a joyful attitude amid their sufferings. Prayer and praise are closely related, and praise is a form of prayer. Many of the great hymns of praise we sing in the church were written as prayers.

Giving praise in trials is not as rare as it might seem. In the first chapter of his epistle, for example, James encouraged his readers, "Consider it all joy, my brothers, when you encounter various trials, knowing that the testing of your faith produces endurance. And let endurance have its perfect result, that you may be mature and complete, lacking in nothing" (James 1:2-4). While joy may not be our initial response, by faith we sing praises for the good things God has promised to accomplish through our trials.

A second truth we see in James's paragraph on prayer is *the link* between *the prayers of the elders of the church and spiritual restoration*. This part of the passage has often been a source of disagreement among students of Scripture. At first glance, it appears that believers who are sick may expect physical healing if they will simply call for the elders of the church and ask for prayer.

While there is certainly nothing wrong about requesting prayer for our physical ailments, the word for *suffering*, as mentioned earlier, is referencing the evil treatment the believers were receiving from an unbelieving, hostile world. This being the case, those referred to as *sick* is almost certainly speaking of those who had grown weary from the hostility and persecution they were facing.

To be fair as we interpret James' words, "there are places in the New Testament, primarily in the Gospels, where the word translated *sick* does refer to physical sickness. But in an almost equal number of places, it refers to spiritual or emotional distress or weakness, not physical sickness."[3] Understanding the needs of those who received this epistle helps us see that this was the nature of the suffering they were experiencing.

James was writing to those who had grown weak and weary in their sufferings, *Christians* who had become discouraged in the spiritual battle, so much so that they were losing their ability to endure. These were fallen spiritual warriors who had grown weary, depressed, and in some cases, defeated. Even though they had relied on God's strength in the beginning, at some point they lost their resolve to continue and fell into sinful attitudes. They became so weak and disheartened that they were unable to pray, and needed the loving, prayerful assistance of others who were more mature in their faith. So, James writes: "Is anyone among you sick (weak)? Then he must call for the elders of the church and they are to pray over him, anointing him with oil in the name of the Lord; and the prayer offered in faith will restore the one who is sick, and the Lord will raise him up, and if he has committed sins, they will be forgiven him" (James 5:14-15).

As I reflect on the condition James is describing, my mind turns to the occupation of shepherding, to a condition shepherds refer to as a *sheep being cast*. Phillip Keller, in his book, *A Shepherd Looks at Psalm 23*, writing of his experience as a shepherd in Kenya, describes this dangerous circumstance: "A sheep may roll on its side slightly to rest or relax. Suddenly the center of gravity in the body shifts so it turns on its back far enough that the feet no longer touch the ground. It may feel a sense of panic and start to paw frantically. Frequently this only makes things worse. It rolls over even further. Now it is quite impossible to regain its feet."[4] Keller goes on to explain the joy of finding a cast sheep before it was too late and lovingly helping that sheep get back on its feet and the road to restored health.

This is much like the experience when elders and others who are more mature in their faith come alongside their weary, suffering fellow-believers – *cast sheep.* The relational principle is one we often see in Scripture: "We who are strong ought to bear the weaknesses of those without strength, and not just please ourselves" (Romans 15:1).

While I have at times joined other elders in anointing people with oil in the name of the Lord as we prayed for their need, many Bible scholars point out that this may not have been a ceremonial anointing at all, but an anointing for medicinal purposes. You may recall Jesus' story of the Good Samaritan who assisted the man who had been robbed, beaten, and left for dead by the side of the road. (See Luke 10:29-37.) The Samaritan also bandaged him up, *pouring in oil* and wine, along with generously providing for his other needs. Some believe this could have been how it was with these suffering believers. Perhaps the elders rubbed their wounds with oil as they lovingly served and prayed for them in the name of the Lord.

When James specifies that the elders were to do this *in the name of the Lord,* the inference is that they were to minister to those who were hurting with the same attitude Jesus would have displayed had He been in the same set of circumstances. Jesus is not only our Savior and Lord; He is also our model and example in relating to and serving those who are in pain and suffering.

The third truth is this: *there is a vital link between praying for one another and spiritual wholeness.* After dealing first with personal prayer, and then to having the elders pray, James turns to this mutual, reciprocal ministry of Christians praying for one another, the primary focus of this chapter. Here are his words: "Confess your sins to one another and pray for one another, so that you may be healed" (James 5:16).

As James writes these words of instruction, he is aware that the spiritually weary believer could be one who had become isolated from others and, therefore, more vulnerable to Satan's attacks. The nature of sin is such that it seeks to remain private, whereas God wants it to be brought out into the open, into the light, where it can be confessed and forsaken. Spiritual health is best maintained when we are connected to other believers, vitally involved in mutually supportive fellowship, and loving accountability. "He who separates himself seeks his own desire; he quarrels against all sound wisdom" (Proverbs 18:1). When we purpose to stay connected to other believers in the way described in the New Testament, the mutually supportive *one another* encounters, so prominent in the New Testament, are much more likely to occur, including praying for one another.

The troublesome part of this verse is the opening phrase, "Confess your sins to one another." The KJV uses the word *faults*, and this is one instance where most would prefer that rendering; faults are much easier to confess than actual sins. But the word is *sin* or *trespass*, and the admonition of Scripture is to confess them to one another and then to pray, requiring a depth of relationship many Christians never experience.

When it comes to the confession of sin, if you are like me, you are going to be especially careful about who you choose to hear your confession. If someone is known for having a loose tongue, being a gossip, or giving a bad report of others, he will not be the person I choose. To confess to one another requires an enormous amount of trust, the kind that is built around a bond of mutual fellowship with our Lord over time.

On various occasions in my years as a pastor, people have confided in me and confessed certain sins. In each case, I felt profoundly humbled that they would put that level of trust in me. In my heart, I knew I was called to faithfully pray that God would bring healing to their lives in His time, even as James states.

There have been times when I too have confessed to others, asking for prayer to be healed of my waywardness and failure to trust and delight in God. The ones who have heard my confessions have been kind and accepting, pointing me to God's grace and forgiveness, and I am deeply thankful.

The fourth and final truth is this: *there is a vital link between the prayers of the righteous and spiritual change.* As James nears the conclusion of his helpful instruction on prayer, to reinforce his point, he writes: "The effective prayer of a righteous man can accomplish much" (James 5:16). The initial response of many is to believe that their prayers could never be effective since they do not see themselves as *righteous.* If we are looking only to ourselves, this is true. The Bible states, "There is none righteous, not even one" (Romans 3:10). What we need to remember, however, is that Christ has become our righteousness. "He made Him who knew no sin to be sin on our behalf, that we might become the righteousness of God in Him" (II Corinthians 5:21). "By His doing you are in Christ Jesus, who became to us wisdom from God, and *righteousness* and sanctification and redemption" (I Corinthians 1:30; italics mine). Each time we pray, we approach God through our Mediator; we pray *in Jesus' name*, as He taught us. (See John 14:13-14.) When we approach our Father in this way, we are affirming that we are coming to Him, not through our merit, but only through the righteousness of Christ, who is our Great High Priest.

James illustrates his point by reminding his readers of the prophet, Elijah. "Elijah was a man with a nature like ours, and he prayed earnestly that it would not rain, and it did not rain on the earth for the space of three years and six months. Then he prayed again, and the sky poured forth rain and the earth produced its fruit" (James 5:17).

Most familiar with the Old Testament remember Elijah as a courageous, fiery prophet who did heroic exploits in his ministry. James, however, reminds us that *Elijah was a man with a nature like ours*, and Scripture makes no attempt to hide this important fact. When the wicked Queen Jezebel threatened to kill him, "he was afraid and arose and ran for his life" (I Kings 19:3). This led to a time of depression and self-pity which he expressed to the Lord: "I have been very zealous for the Lord, the God of hosts; for the sons of Israel have forsaken Your covenant, torn down Your altars and killed Your prophets with the sword. And I alone am left; and they seek my life to take it away" (I Kings 19:10). On these occasions, Elijah could have been viewed as a *cast sheep*, such as Phillip Keller described.

The encouraging point James is making, however, is that even *with a nature like ours – a flawed human nature,* his prayers set in motion a severe drought of three and a half years, and his prayers ended it as well. John MacArthur, in his commentary on James, shares an interesting insight into the nature of this miracle James chose for his readers. "The story of Elijah and the drought would certainly be a strange illustration if James had physical illness and healing in view throughout this passage. Certainly, there are numerous biblical illustrations of healing from which he could have drawn. But the picture of rain pouring down on parched ground perfectly illustrates God's outpouring of spiritual blessings on the dry and parched souls of struggling believers. And He does both in response to the righteous prayers of godly people."[5]

In summary, there are times when we plead and cry out to God in our sufferings, other occasions when we call for the elders of the church, or other mature believers, to lift us to the Father in prayer. But there are also circumstances when we find a trusted brother or sister in Christ and confess to them some life-dominating sin, and then humbly ask for prayer.

Before my mother died at the age of 90, she would sometimes say to me, *"I don't know if my old prayers do much good anymore or not."* Based on this passage, and many others which reinforce the power of prayer, I assured her that they did, and I am confident they still do, even though God called her home some years ago.

Chapter Fifteen Discussion Questions

1. Read again Phillip Yancey's quote on prayer in the first paragraph of the chapter. How have you found this to be true in your friendships with those for whom you have prayed?
2. What lessons do we learn from the way Jesus made prayer such a high priority, even though He was the Son of God?
3. To what extent can you identify with the type of suffering and spiritual weariness James's readers was experiencing?
4. What are the spiritual lessons of the *cast sheep* described by Phillip Keller? Why is it that we as God's sheep at times find ourselves in this same predicament?
5. What qualities are needed to become a friend to whom others would feel free to confess their sins?
6. What lessons about prayer can we learn from the prophet, Elijah?
7. What are some practical steps we can take to be more deliberate in praying for our brothers and sisters in Christ?
8. What is one application you hope to take away from this chapter?

Chapter Sixteen

Serve One Another

"As each one has received a special gift, employ it in serving one another as good stewards of the manifold grace of God."

I Peter 4:10

All serious students of Scripture are aware that God has a precise plan for each of His children, one that was predetermined in eternity past, namely, to make us like His Son, the Lord Jesus Christ. Many can also quote the hopeful verse, "And we know that God causes all things to work together for good to those who love God, to those who are called according to His purpose" (Romans 8:28). As amazing as it is, like a master-weaver God is using *all things* in our lives for this grand purpose: we are "predestined to be conformed to the image of His Son" (Romans 8:29).

While much time could be spent searching the Scriptures to discover what it means to be *conformed to the image of His Son,* Jesus' own words provide a wonderful starting point: "For the Son of Man did not come to be served, but to serve, and to give His life as a ransom for many" (Mark 10:45). In commenting on this verse, Charles R. Swindoll writes, "After bringing us into His family through faith in His Son, the Lord Jesus Christ, God sets His sights on building into us the same quality that made Jesus distinct from all others of His day. He is engaged in building into His people the same serving and giving qualities that characterized His Son."[1]

Servanthood was a recurring theme in the teaching of Jesus, but a truth His disciples were slow to learn. On more than one

185

occasion they argued among themselves as to who was the greatest. The mother of James and John even came to Jesus requesting that her sons be granted the honor of sitting next to Him when His kingdom was established. Jesus' immediate response was startling, "You do not know what you are asking. Are you able to drink the cup I am about to drink? (Matthew 20:22) While they responded that they were able, Jesus bluntly informed them of the persecution and suffering they would soon experience as His followers. He also explained that the decision of who would sit next to Him in His future kingdom was not His to make.

Having been part of that unforgettable exchange, Matthew was careful to record the response of the others to the appeal by the mother of James and John: "And hearing this, the ten became indignant with the two brothers" (Matthew 20:24). As Charles Swindoll states, "There was no way they were going to give up those top spots without a fight."[2]

Seeing this as a teachable moment, Jesus immediately gave them an unforgettable lesson on servanthood, one that has application in the church throughout all generations. "Jesus called them to Himself and said, 'You know that the rulers of the Gentiles lord it over them, and their great men exercise authority over them. It is not this way among you, but whoever wishes to become great among you shall be your servant, and whoever wishes to be first among you shall be your slave; just as the Son of Man did not come to be served, but to serve, and to give His life a ransom for many" (Matthew 20:25-28). Astonishingly, Jesus took the management structure utilized throughout the entire secular world and turned it upside down, giving His followers an entirely new paradigm for Christian leadership. Those with a true servant's heart would be considered greatest in the kingdom, while those with domineering, lording-it-over attitudes were to have no place among His followers.

186

When Jesus chose this struggling group of men to be His apostles, He saw them for who they were, but He also envisioned who they would become as a result of the three years of training they would receive from being with Him. He also knew of the character-transforming work of the Holy Spirit which they would come to experience, enabling ordinary men to become His extraordinary, faithful servants.

Other than at the cross, at no other point in Jesus' life was His servanthood on greater display than during the final Passover meal He shared with His disciples, only hours before the cross. Due to another of their petty arguments as to who was the greatest, His disciples failed to arrange for a servant to be present to wash the dusty and dirty feet of those present at the meal. To the shock and bewilderment of the entire group, "Jesus got up from supper, and laid aside His garments; and taking a towel, He girded Himself. Then He poured water into the basin and began to wash the disciples' feet and to wipe them with the towel with which He was girded" (John 13:4-5). The MacArthur Study Bible provides this helpful insight: "Although the disciples most likely would have been happy to wash Jesus' feet, they could not conceive of washing one another's feet. This was because in the society at that time foot-washing was reserved for the lowliest of menial servants."[3] This explains why they were completely stunned when Jesus, choosing to take the role of a lowly servant, humbly washed their feet, despite Peter's initial insistence that it would never happen. Interestingly, Jesus also washed the feet of Judas, though He was aware that he would betray Him later that very evening.

Once Jesus completed His lowly task, it was time to explain the meaning of what He had done. "So, when He had washed their feet, and taken His garments and reclined at the table again, He said to them, 'Do you know what I have done to you? You call me Teacher and Lord; and you are right, for so I am. If I then, the Lord and Teacher, washed your feet, you also ought to wash one another's

187

feet. For I gave you an example that you should also do as I did to you. Truly, truly I say to you, a slave is not above his master, nor is one who is sent greater than the one who sent him. If you know these things, you are blessed if you do them'" (John 13:12-17).

While some groups have taken Jesus' words literally, establishing foot washing *as* a ritual in the church, nothing in the New Testament suggests that this was what Jesus intended. The correct perspective is to view His loving actions as an unforgettable lesson in how His followers were to serve one another, in whatever form the need may present itself. While Jesus promised a blessing to those who would obediently practice what He had taught, being a servant is never easy. Most of us prefer to be served, rather than thinking of how we can lovingly meet the needs of others; if we do serve, most of us want to be applauded for our noble deed.

The poet, Ruth Harms Calkin, creatively captures how many Christians approach any opportunity to serve others. While written from the perspective as a woman, her poem, entitled, "I Wonder", has application for us all.

You know, Lord, how I serve You
With great emotional fervor
In the limelight.
You know how eagerly I speak for You
At a woman's club.
You know how I effervesce when I promote
A fellowship group.
You know my genuine enthusiasm
At a Bible study.

But how would I react, I wonder
If You pointed to a basin of water
And asked me to wash the calloused feet

Of a bent and wrinkled old woman
Day after day
Month after month
In a room where nobody saw
And nobody knew.[4]

Some years ago, while conducting the funeral of an elderly woman in our church in Tyler, Texas, I chose to use this poem as part of my sermon. The lady who died had been a great blessing in her younger years to everyone who knew her. In her declining years, however, after her husband died and she was facing deteriorating health, she became difficult, even impossible, to please, becoming agitated at everything and everyone who tried to assist. Despite the enormous challenge it was to serve her, three precious women in our church continued to faithfully meet her needs, day after day, month after month, doing so without complaint or any desire for recognition. Because I was aware of their devoted service in extremely difficult circumstances, the insightful words in Ruth Harms Calkin's poem aptly captured what needed to be communicated.

My experience is that while those in the church with a true servant's heart appreciate a sincere word of appreciation, most feel uncomfortable when they are recognized. They have learned the lesson God is seeking to teach all His children; our service is to be done to *an audience of One, the Lord Jesus Christ.* His is the example we are seeking to follow, and He is the Master we are called to please.

A wonderful example of this truth is in the Apostle Paul's letter to the church in Philippi. There is evidence that this instructive passage became one of the early hymns of the church. In it the Apostle Paul describes the essence of true servanthood, lifting up Jesus as our incomparable example: "Do nothing from selfishness or empty conceit, but with humility of mind regard one another as more important than yourselves; do not merely look out for your own personal interests, but also for the interests of others. Let this attitude be in you which was also in Christ Jesus, who although He existed in the form of God, did not regard equality with God a thing to be grasped, but emptied Himself, *taking the form of a bond-servant*, and being made in the likeness of men. Being found in appearance as a man, He humbled Himself by becoming obedient to the point of death, even death on a cross" (Philippians 2:3-8; italics mine).

What we see in this astonishing passage is the self-emptying our Lord displayed in the Incarnation. He who was eternally God, while still maintaining His divine attributes, willingly laid them aside to take on all the essential attributes of humanity. In coming to us, He also *took the form of a lowly bondservant*, submitting Himself to the will of His Father, and the leading of the Holy Spirit, demonstrating obedience to the point of death on the cross. At the heart of Paul's words of application is that we as Christians are to have the same attitude in ourselves that we see in Christ, that of a serving and giving bondservant who places the needs and interests of others ahead of our own.

If we see the issue correctly, serving is not so much what we do as it is who we are. Paul, Timothy, Peter, James, and Jude all referred to themselves as *bondservants* of Jesus Christ, viewing themselves entirely at His disposal, knowing He was their Master.

In Roman times, a bondservant could refer to one who voluntarily served others, though it most often referred to one who was a servant permanently. Bondservants were considered the owner's personal property. Romans slaves had no rights and were under the complete control of their masters.

When the apostles referred to themselves as bondservants of Christ, they were likely thinking of the Hebrew word which described a servant who became one voluntarily, after having been won by the gracious treatment he received from his master. Under Mosaic Law a provision was made for servants who served six years to be set free in the seventh, but also for them to remain with their master, should they choose to do so. "If a slave plainly says, 'I love my master, my wife, and my children; I will not go out as a free man,' then his master shall bring him before God, then he shall bring him to the door or the doorpost. And his master shall pierce his ear with an awl, and he shall serve him permanently'" (Exodus 21:5-6). From that point on, that servant was viewed as a *love slave.*

It appears that the apostles had this lovely picture in mind when they described their spiritual identity as bondservants. They knew they had been set free by their Lord Jesus Christ, but saw themselves as His servants because of love. God's plan is that we also view ourselves in this way, because as Paul says, "You are not your own, for you have been bought with a price: therefore glorify God in your body" (I Corinthians 6:19-20).

We see this identical truth in Paul's letter to the Galatians: "For you were called to freedom, brethren; only do not turn your freedom into an opportunity for the flesh, but through love serve one another" (Galatians 5:13). In this case, however, Paul's admonition is not about serving Christ, but serving one another. The point is clear, however; when we serve one another in love, we are also serving Christ. Jesus made this clear in the concluding words of one of His most famous parables: "Truly I say to you, to the extent that you did it to one of these brothers of Mine, even to the least of them, you did it to Me" (Matthew 25:40).

In writing of how the Apostle Paul saw himself as a servant of Christ, but also a servant to others, Gene Getz explains, "Some

Christians stop at this point, not realizing that being *a servant of Christ* also involves them with other members of the Body of Christ. Turning our lives over to Christ also means turning our lives over to each other. We are part of a body of which Christ is the head. Being 'in Christ' also means being 'a part of each other'".[5]

An essential truth to learn about servanthood is that God has given each member of His body at least one spiritual gift to faithfully exercise for the overall health of the church. While we see spiritual gifts spoken of at different points in the New Testament, the Apostle Peter provides this helpful summary: "As each one has received a special gift, employ it in serving one another as good stewards of the manifold grace of God. Whoever speaks, let him speak as it were the utterances of God; whoever serves is to do so as one serving by the strength which God supplies; so that in all things God may be glorified through Jesus Christ, to whom belongs the glory and dominion forever and ever" (I Peter 4:10-11). Along with affirming that *each one has received a special gift,* Peter separates the gifts into two broad, helpful categories: *speaking and serving.* This means that some acts of service will be more noticeable, while others are carried out behind the scenes. In either case, they were to be *employed in serving one another*, the theme of this chapter. In the ultimate sense of the word, each gift was meant to bring glory to God, and never to ourselves.

Much of Jesus' training was to help His followers embrace their identity as His servants. In one of His parables Christians often overlook, Jesus unforgettably made this point: "Which of you, having a slave plowing or tending sheep, will say to him when he has come in from the field, 'Come immediately and sit down to eat'? But will he not say to him, 'Prepare something for me to eat, and properly clothe yourself and serve me while I eat and drink, and afterward you may eat or drink'? He does not thank that slave because he did the things which were commanded, does he? So you too, when you do all the things you are commanded you, say, '*We are unworthy slaves; we have done only that which we ought to have done'"* (Luke 17:7-10; italics mine).

Sadly, in our flesh and spiritual immaturity, most crave the limelight and attention, even if we are serving in the smallest capacity. The intent of Jesus' parable is to help us deal with any expectations we might have about recognition; instead, He intends for us to simply focus on serving Him because of who He is, and who we are as His servants, and not for the praise and applause of men.

In the early years of my Christian life, my pastor took me in the summers to some of the old fashioned, ten-day camp meetings with three services each day, along with two youth services. As a new Christian, eager to grow in my faith and knowledge of the Bible, I loved the sermons. One of the eloquent itinerant preachers told the story of a missionary and his wife who were returning by ship to America after a lifetime of service in Africa. Because of poor health, the mission board informed them it was time for them to retire. Onboard that same ship President Teddy Roosevelt was returning from a hunting safari with several companions. When the ship arrived, a large crowd was waiting on shore with bands playing, and balloons floating in the air in colorful array. The people cheered as they welcomed home their president. When it came time for the elderly missionary couple to slowly make their way down the now quiet gangplank alone to the empty docks, with no one to welcome or affirm them for their years of service, there was an understandable sense of discouragement. Sensing her husband's inner disappointment, his godly wife took his hand and whispered in his ear, *"We're not home yet!"*

This is a truth all servants of Christ must keep in mind. As long as God chooses to keep us here, we are to faithfully carry out the ministry tasks assigned to us, seeking to do as the Apostle Paul instructed the first-century slaves: "Whatever you do, do your work heartily, as for the Lord, rather than for men, knowing that from the

Lord you will receive the reward of your inheritance. It is the Lord Christ whom you serve" (Colossians 3:23-24).

While we know that our entrance into heaven when God calls us home will only be by His grace, based on what the Lord Jesus Christ has accomplished for us, and not our works; our desire, nevertheless, is to please Him in our service. There is a longing in the heart of every believer to one day hear from Him the encouraging words, "Well done, you good and faithful servant...enter into the joy of your master" (Matthew 25:23 ESV[6]).

Chapter Sixteen Discussion Questions

1. Knowing God plans to make us like Jesus, who came among us as the Servant, how can we best cooperate with His plan and embrace more of a servant's attitude?
2. What are the primary lessons to be gained from Jesus washing the feet of His disciples?
3. How can we overcome the desire for recognition and simply serve from the heart to please our Lord?
4. How are Christians today like the love-slaves in the Old Testament who chose to stay with their master?
5. What part do spiritual gifts play in discovering our place of service in the church?
6. How can we help our brothers and sisters in Christ to embrace the truth that we are serving Christ when we serve one another?
7. The words, "Well done, good and faithful servant" are ones we all long to hear. What attitudes and actions are needed to receive this beautiful commendation from our Lord?

Chapter Seventeen
Comfort One Another

"Therefore, comfort one another with these words."

I Thessalonians 4:18

When Jesus delivered His Sermon on the Mount near the beginning of His ministry, one of the first issues He addressed was that of comfort: "Blessed are those who mourn, for they shall be comforted" (Matthew 5:4). To be human is to mourn, for we live in a fallen world. The goods news promised by Jesus is that those who mourn will be comforted, the issue we will explore in this chapter.

In his book, *The Four Loves,* C. S. Lewis astutely observed, "To love anything at all is to be vulnerable. Love anything and your heart will be wrung and possibly broken. If you want to make sure of keeping your heart intact, you must give it to no one, not even a pet."[1]

If we experience grief following the loss of a pet, and we know we do, how much greater the sorrow when the departed one is our spouse, our child, a parent or grandparent, our sister or brother, or a cherished friend in Christ? To love another person is to put ourselves in a vulnerable position, for when they are gone from us, we grieve, experiencing a deep sense of loss.

To experience grief is an integral part of being human; we grieve because we are created in the image of God. How comforting to know that our Lord Himself was described as "a man of sorrows and acquainted with grief" and that "He bore our griefs and carried our sorrows" (Isaiah 53:3,4). Grief is a common experience in families and friendships, as it was with Jesus. We remember Him weeping at the graveside of His friend, Lazarus (John 11:35), as He shared in the sorrow of his sisters, Mary and Martha, even though He would soon raise Lazarus from the dead. Grief is not a sign of weakness, nor is it a lack of faith; it is simply the price of love.

This is the issue addressed by the Apostle Paul in his first letter to the church at Thessalonica. These first-century believers understood that Jesus had promised to return, and they anticipated His return to be soon, even in their lifetimes. But as Jesus delayed, some in the church began to die. Those who remained had questions and concerns about their loved ones. What would happen to family members and friends who had departed before the Lord returned? Would those who had died miss out on His climactic return? Would those who were still alive when He returned have an advantage over their fellow believers who had died? These are the issues Paul addresses in I Thessalonians 4:13-18. It was a most instructive paragraph for the first century Christians, but for believers in all generations as well. It concludes with this statement: "Therefore, comfort one another with these words" (I Thessalonians 4:18). What truths did Paul communicate in this brief paragraph to give comfort, truths they could then use in comforting one another?

His instruction began with these words: "We do not want you to be uninformed, brothers, about those who are asleep, so that you do not grieve as the rest who have no hope" (I Thessalonians 4:13). Comfort, the type that enabled them to grieve with hope, resided in the comprehensive truths Paul communicated to them.

Sleep, the word selected by Paul, was the term used at times in the Bible to describe when life had gone out of the body. The physical body is our temporary dwelling place during our stay on earth; it is our earthly tent or earth suit. When the Bible refers to death as sleep, this refers only to the body, not to the spirit. We know from Scripture that when physical life is gone and the person is pronounced dead, those who are believers in Christ go immediately to be with Him. The Apostle Paul affirms this in his second letter to the church in Corinth: "To be absent from the body is to be at home with the Lord" (II Corinthians 5:8).

Paul expressed this identical truth in his letter to the church in Philippi, explaining the dilemma he was facing at that time: "If I am to live on in the flesh, this will mean fruitful labor for me; and I do not know which to choose. But I am hard-pressed from both directions, having the desire *to depart and be with Christ,* for that is far better, yet to remain on in the flesh is more necessary for your sake" (Philippians 1:22-24; italics mine). Paul understood that to depart from his body at death meant being with Christ, which he stated was *far better.* The summary of his position is beautifully captured in these words: "For to me, to live is Christ, and to die is gain" (Philippians 1:21).

Paul's primary concern was that the believers in Thessalonica *would not grieve as the rest who had no hope.* To assure that they would instead *grieve with hope,* Paul gave them the truth, God's divine revelation, to answer their questions and as the antidote to their grief. Paul understood Jesus' words, "You shall know the truth, and the truth will set you free" (John 8:32). Truth, in this instance, set the troubled believers free from grieving without hope, as others do who are without Christ.

It is significant to note that Paul did not reprimand them for their grief; he simply acknowledged that grief over the departure of loved ones was understandable. It is normal and appropriate to experience sorrow when loved ones die and pass from our sight. Paul's approach was to share the truth that would bring them comfort. The phrase we will explore in this chapter is "these words" in I Thessalonians 4:18, referring to words of truth Paul knew would bring them comfort, enabling them *to grieve with hope*, and to *comfort one another.*

Paul's brief but power-packed paragraph contains five reassuring truths, all interrelated. My plan in this chapter is to utilize five words skillfully employed by Warren Wiersbe in *The Bible Exposition Commentary,* along with an explanatory phrase for each one.[2]

The first is REVELATION – *God has given us His truth.* Paul's introductory statement is this, "This we say to you by the word of the Lord...." (I Thessalonians 4:15). Revelation calls attention to Paul's insistence that the truths he was writing to the church were not his own, but words of comfort he had received *by the word of the Lord.*

How blessed we are that God has given within His Word a definitive word about death and what happens afterward. What a sharp contrast this is when compared to human wisdom, which offers little more than speculations about what happens to people after they die. Philosophers through the ages have also wrestled with the question of immortality. Those in the occult world are known by attempts to connect with those who have died. Others endeavor to explain and clarify the near-death, or after death experiences of those who have returned, whose stories quickly become best sellers. What we see in their accounts is a lack of consistency in their speculative, subjective answers, no ring of truth about what they are saying. In contrast to these conflicting stories is the timeless truth of the Word of God.

The truth of what happens after death is progressively revealed in Scripture, but in such a way that each new piece of information is consistent with what came before, so there is no contradiction. In the Book of Job, for example, is the account of a man who lived sometime before Abraham, but after Noah and the flood. Amid his horrendous suffering and loss, Job reflected about death, once asking, "If a man dies, shall he live again?" (Job 14:14) Interestingly, only a few chapters later, Job answered *the* very question he asked, and his words are a significant part of the revelation of God about death and what happens next. "Oh that my words were written! Oh that they were inscribed in a book! That with an iron pen and lead they were engraved in the rock forever! For I know that My Redeemer lives, and at the last He will stand upon the earth. And after my skin has been destroyed, yet in my flesh I will see God, whom I shall see for myself, and my eyes shall behold, and not another" (Job 19:23-27). In the margin of one of my Bibles I have written: *Job – Your words are written in a book – God's book!* Though the book that bears his name includes some of the earliest histories in the Bible, Job's description of what happens after death is a significant part of the answer, and consistent with all that follows.

God's revelation on this issue, as we know, climaxed in the coming of Jesus into the world. We first see this in His teaching and in His miracles. One example where the two come together is when Jesus' friend, Lazarus, died, and his body had been in the tomb four days before Jesus arrived. In giving comfort to Mary and Martha, the devoted sisters of Lazarus, even tenderly weeping with them, Jesus informed them that their brother would rise again. Martha responded by affirming her faith that her brother would rise again in the last day. Jesus then said to her, "I am the resurrection and the life; he who believes in Me will live even if he dies, and everyone who lives and believes in Me will never die. Do you believe this?" (John 11:25-26) To demonstrate His power, Jesus walked out to the grave and cried with a loud voice, "Lazarus, come forth!" (John 11:43) Lazarus immediately came forth, still wrapped in his grave clothes. Jesus then instructed his friends to assist Lazarus in freeing himself from the clothes he no longer needed. Jesus had declared His power over death, but He also dramatically demonstrated it.

Commenting on this passage, one of the ancient Puritan preachers suggested that it was a good thing Jesus used the name of

Lazarus when He called him forth and did not simply say "Come forth", or the entire cemetery would have emptied![3]

As great as the miracle of Lazarus was, he would one day die again. The greatest of all miracles, however, is the one on which the veracity of Christianity is based - Jesus' own resurrection, one He had often foretold to His followers. The Apostle Paul describes the significance of Jesus' resurrection in his second letter to Timothy: "He saved us and called us with a holy calling, not according to our works, but according to His purpose and grace which was granted us in Christ Jesus from all eternity, but has now been revealed by the appearing of our Savior, Jesus Christ, *who abolished death and brought life and immortality to light through the gospel*" (II Timothy 1:9-10; italics mine).

The revelation of what happens at death became clear when Jesus abolished death and brought life and immortality to light through the gospel. The distinctive truth of Scripture is that there is an inseparable link between Christ's resurrection and our own. "Now if Christ is preached that He is raised from the dead, how do some among you say that there is no resurrection from the dead? But if there is no resurrection of the dead, not even Christ has been raised; and if Christ has not been raised, then our preaching is vain, and your faith is also in vain" (For the full explanation, see I Corinthians 15:12-20).

The point again is that when Paul writes to the troubled believers in Thessalonica, the comforting truths he shares were revealed to him by *the word of the Lord*.

The second truth is RETURN – *Christ has promised to come again!* The return of Christ, as mentioned earlier, is quite prominent in Paul's letter to the church in Thessalonica. He first references it in the opening chapter, thanking God for their conversion and how they had "turned to God from idols to serve a living and true God, and *to wait for His Son from heaven,* whom He raised from the dead, that is Jesus, who rescues us from the wrath to come chapter" (I Thessalonians 1:9-10; italics mine). In the second, he again writes, "For who is our hope or joy or crown of exultation? Is it not you, in the presence of our Lord Jesus Christ *at His coming?* (I Thessalonians 2:19; italics mine) In the third chapter, he again returns to this theme: "May the Lord cause you to increase and abound in love for one another and for all people...so that He may establish your hearts without blame in holiness before our God and Father *at the coming of our Lord Jesus Christ with all the saints"* (I Thessalonians 3:12-13; italics mine). Because they viewed Christ's return as imminent, they were troubled because of His delay, especially as they saw that their loved ones were dying.

Even so, Paul uses the promise of the Lord's return as one of the prominent truths in his message of comfort. "For if we believe that Jesus died and rose again, even so God will bring with Him those who have fallen asleep in Jesus...we who are alive and remain until *the coming of the Lord* shall not precede those who have fallen asleep in Jesus. *For the Lord Himself will descend from heaven with a shout, with the voice of the archangel, with the trumpet of God* (I Thessalonians 4:14-16; italics mine).

Note again how Paul uses the word *sleep* in referring to believers who have died. He did not say, however, that the spirit or soul of believers went to sleep at death. Rather, he makes it clear that "God will bring with Him those who have fallen asleep in Jesus." It would be impossible to bring them unless they were already with Him, as the passage states. It is not the soul or spirit who sleeps, only the body. It is interesting that James, albeit in a different context, gives the biblical definition of death in his epistle: "...the body without the spirit is dead" (James 2:26). Though the body is dead, the spirit of believers is very much alive, as we will soon see.

At death, the spirit leaves the body, and the body goes to sleep; it no longer functions. The spirit of believers goes to be with the Lord at the very moment of death. Paul makes this clear in other passages, such as this one: "While we are at home in the body we are absent from the Lord - for we walk by faith and not by sight – we are of good courage, I say, and prefer to be *absent from the body and at home with the Lord*" (II Corinthians 5:6-8; italics mine). Of all the biblical pictures of the glorious future that awaits us as believers, *being absent from the body and at home with the Lord*, is one of the most attractive and inviting! Knowing this, it is certainly understandable why Paul, in anticipating this time, *preferred to be absent from the body and to be at home with the Lord.* But there is more comfort!

Third, RESURRECTION – *Christians who die will rise again.* Paul continues his words of comfort by writing: "For the Lord Himself will descend from heaven with a shout, with the voice of the archangel, and with the trumpet of God, and *the dead in Christ shall rise first*" (I Thessalonians 4:16; italics mine).

The astonishing truth here is that as our spirits are reunited with our bodies, they will not be the decaying bodies we had before. What we will receive at this grand moment described by Paul is the new resurrection body our Lord has for us! "But now Christ has been raised, *the first fruits of those who have fallen asleep*" (I Corinthians 15:20; italics mine). The MacArthur Study Bible explains, "This speaks of the first installment of the harvest to eternal life, in which Christ's resurrection will precipitate and guarantee that all of the saints who have died will be resurrected also."[3]

Note that when the Lord returns, and immediately before that moment when we as Christians receive our new bodies, three events will occur simultaneously: *a shout, the voice of the archangel, and the trumpet of God,* followed by, as Paul writes, "the dead in Christ will rise first" (I Thessalonians 4:16). What an amazing, one-time historical event this will be!

In his informative chapter of Christ's resurrection and its significance, Paul wonderfully describes the glorious difference between our old bodies and the new ones we will receive. "But I say this, brothers, that flesh and blood cannot enter the kingdom of God, nor does the perishable inherit the imperishable. Behold, I tell you a mystery; we will not all sleep, but we will all be changed, in a moment, in the twinkling of an eye, at the last trumpet; for the perishable must put on the imperishable, and this mortal must put on immortality. But when this perishable will have put on the imperishable, and this mortal will have put on immortality, then will come about the saying that is written, 'DEATH IS SWALLOWED UP IN VICTORY. O DEATH, WHERE IS YOUR STING? O GRAVE, WHERE IS YOUR VICTORY?'" (I Corinthians 15:50-55)

In the verses that are capitalized here, Paul is quoting from the minor prophet, Hosea, another reminder of the progressive revelation about death and what happens afterward. While life and immortality did not come into its fullest bloom until the time when Christ brought life and immortality to light through the gospel, the seeds were being sown all along, and Hosea is cited as one of those instances.

The fourth word is RAPTURE – *Believers living when Christ returns will be caught up!* While it is incredible news that the dead in Christ will rise first when the shout comes from heaven, along with the voice of the archangel and the trumpet of God, more extraordinary news remains: "And the dead in Christ will rise first. Then we who are alive and remain will be *caught up* together with them to meet the Lord in the air..." (I Thessalonians 4:16-17; italics mine).

It is important to understand that the word *rapture* is not used in this section or in the New Testament, but this is the literal meaning of the phrase – *caught up*. Dr. Kenneth Wuest, a highly respected Greek scholar, has a fascinating explanation of the various word pictures associated with this phrase – *caught up.*[4]

- *To catch away speedily* – The same phrase is used to describe Phillip being unexpectedly *caught up* after having shared the gospel with the Ethiopian. (Acts 8:39) So it will be when the Lord returns in the air; believers on the earth at that time will be *caught away speedily*, in the twinkling of the eye. May God help us to live with greater awareness of this heartening truth.

- *To seize by force* – This is the phrase used in John 6:15 when Jesus saw that His followers were intending to come and *seize Him by force* to make Him king. Could it be that some believers will be so attached to this world that they will *be seized by force* at the rapture, much like Lot was rescued from the wicked city of Sodom? (See Genesis 19:16)

- *To claim for one's self* – This phrase views the rapture from our Lord's point of view as He comes to claim His bride. A song by Acappella pictures that delightful moment when the Father will say to the Son, "Jesus, go and get your bride; today's Your wedding day."[5]

- *To move to a new place* – This phrase reminds us of Jesus' reassuring words just before the cross, "I go to prepare a place for you. If I go to prepare a place for you, I will come again, and receive you unto Myself, that where I am, there you may be also" (John 14:2-3). Yes, when our Lord returns for His church, we will *move to a new place, our Father's house!*

- *To rescue from danger* – This phrase is used in Acts 23:22-24 when the Apostle Paul was on trial. One of the commanders learned that Paul was in danger, fearing he would be torn to pieces. The commander ordered his troops to go and take Paul by force and bring him into the barracks, *rescuing him from danger.*

Words fail us in attempting to describe how incredible it would be if we are blessed to be part of that generation of Christians who will be *caught up* and raptured away when our Lord returns! This grand event which will occur "in a moment, in the twinkling of an eye, at the last trumpet" (I Corinthians 15:52), will be unlike anything that has come before or will occur afterward.

The fifth word is REUNION – *All believers will be with their Lord forever!* The most comforting phrase in this instructive, hope-filled passage may very well be – "And so we shall always be with the Lord" (I Thessalonians 4:17). While our eternal future includes infinitely more than our finite minds can fathom, being forever with our Savior and Redeemer will far surpass every other delight!

In this passage, however, Paul also answers one of the most pressing questions of the church, namely, *will we see again our loved ones who have died?* Note carefully Paul's explanation, "The Lord will bring with Him those who have fallen asleep in Jesus...we who are alive and remain until the coming of the Lord will not precede those who have fallen asleep...and the dead in Christ will rise first, then we who are alive and remain will be caught up *together with them* in the clouds, to meet the Lord in the air, and so we shall always be with the Lord" (I Thessalonians 4:14, 17; italics mine). If we are honored to be part of that generation when Christ returns for His church, this means that we will be *caught up* with those whose bodies have died, but whose spirits have been with Jesus. All of us together will receive our resurrection bodies in a joyful, eternal reunion of God's forever family, and so *we shall always be with the Lord.*

Reviewing the incredible truths in this paragraph enables us to understand why the Apostle Paul, for purposes of the application, would conclude as he did: "Therefore, comfort one another with these words" (I Thessalonians 4:18). Nothing brings comfort to grieving hearts of believers as much as the truth of God's Word. Because of the deep love those in the church had for their loved ones whose bodies had died, they would still grieve, but not as those who have no hope. Biblical hope enables us to grieve with hope, and what difference this is!

With these truths about death and eternity fresh in our minds, I would like to ask a personal question: *Have you come to the place in your spiritual journey where you know for certain that if you were to die before the day is out, you would go to heaven?* As I have asked that question to many over the years, I have received a variety of answers. Some respond with a definite "yes" while others have simply said "no". Still others reply, *"I hope so"* or, *"I think so",* and still others have responded, *"I don't think you can know."*

When the Apostle John was concluding his gospel, he stated his purpose for writing, one that addresses this issue of knowing and being sure about one's salvation, "Many other signs Jesus performed in the presence of His disciples, which are not written in this book; but these have been written so that you might believe that Jesus is the Christ, the Son of God, and that believing you might have life in His name" (John 20:30-31). When we turn to his epistle written near the end of his life, John returns to this same theme: "And the testimony is this, that God has given to us eternal life, and this life is in His Son. He who has the Son has the life; he who does not have the Son of God does not have the life. These things I have written to you who believe in the name of the Son of God, *so that you may know that you have eternal life*" (I John 5:11-13; italics mine).

The Bible clearly states that it is possible to know where we stand with God, with this being one of the prominent reasons why the Bible was written. Scripture also makes it clear that salvation is not something we will ever be righteous enough to obtain or achieve through our good deeds or merit. As the Apostle John stated, "God has given to us eternal life, and this life is in His Son." We receive this gift of Jesus, and along with Him - eternal life - by humbly opening our hearts to Him in response to His gracious call, and placing our faith in Him alone for our salvation.

To illustrate what it means to trust in Christ alone for our eternal salvation, I often tell the story I first heard from Dr. D. James Kennedy. An old Scottish lady was dying, and as was the custom in those days, the pastor came by to see if the person had true faith. As she lay dying on her bed, he asked, "Do you still trust Christ?" "Ah, yes I do," she said, "He is my only hope in life and death." The pastor then asked, "Do you believe He will take you to heaven?" "Yes, I know He will," she replied. The pastor then inquired, "But what if He does not take you to heaven?" The woman paused only for a moment and then replied, "Ah, God may do what He wills, but if He does not take me to heaven, He will lose more than I. Though I will lose my soul, He will lose His honor, for He has promised that those who trust in His Son will never perish."[5]

This elderly woman's unwavering testimony reveals what it means to trust Christ alone for our eternal salvation. I hope your trust is in Him as well. "For by grace you have been saved through faith; and that not of yourselves, it is the gift of God; not as a result of works, lest anyone should boast" (Ephesians 2:8-9).

Chapter Seventeen Discussion Questions

1. What is it like to grieve without hope? Have you observed this in others? What are some of the differences when someone grieves with hope?
2. We remember the words of Jesus, "You shall know the truth and the truth will set you free" (John 8:32). What are the truths that set us free from grieving without hope?
3. Discuss the truths Paul gave to his troubled friends in the church at Thessalonica. What are some of the ways these same truths enable us to comfort one another today?
4. What is our only hope in life and in death? How is it possible that we were blessed to hear and respond to the Gospel? What were some of the things God did to make it possible?
5. How can we know and be sure that we have eternal life? While each person's story will be different, what do all salvation testimonies have in common?

Notes

Chapter One

1. Gene Getz, *Sharpening the Focus of the Church*, 62.
2. Jerry Bridges, *True Fellowship*, 14.
3. J.I. Packer, *God's Words*, 191.
4. Bridges, *True Fellowship*, 16.
5. *The New English Bible*, I John 1:3.
6. Packer, *God's Words,* 193.
7. Ibid, 196.
8. Bridges, *True Fellowship,* 20.
9. Dietrich Bonhoeffer, *Life Together*, 20.
10. John MacArthur, *MacArthur Study Bible*, comment on I Corinthians 12:13.

Chapter Two

1. Gene Getz, *Loving One Another*, 21.
2. Merrill Tenney, *John, the Gospel of Belief,* 199.
3. Getz, *Loving One Another*, 22.
4. Francis A. Schaeffer, *The Mark of the Christian*, 13.
5. J. Warren Smith, "See How These Christians Love one Another."
6. Gene Getz, *Sharpening the Focus of the Church*, 113.

Chapter Three

1. John Piper, "The Holy Kiss – Relevant Today or Not?"
2. Alexander Strauch, *The Hospitality Commands*, 7.
3. Henry Blackaby, *Experiencing God – Knowing and Doing the Will of God*, 17.

Chapter Four

1. *New King James Version*, Ephesians 1:5-6.
2. John MacArthur, *MacArthur Study Bible,* comment on Romans 14:1.

Chapter Five

1. *Authorized King James Version,* Galatians 6:5.
2. *New International Version,* Galatians 5:25.
3. William Barclay, *Daily Study Bible: Letters to the Galatians and Ephesians,* p. 58.

Chapter Six

1. Gene Getz, *Building up one Another,* 21.
2. *The Living Bible*, I Corinthians 13:7.
3. Getz, *Building up one Another,* 22.
4. Ibid, 23.

Chapter Seven

1. Alexander Strauch, *The Hospitality Commands*, 5.
2. Rosario Butterfield, *The Gospel Comes with a House Key,* 14.
3. Strauch, *The Hospitality Commands,* 7.
4. *English Standard Version Bible,* Romans 12:13.
5. Charles M. Schultz, *Happiness is a Warm Blanket,* 6.
6. Strauch, *The Hospitality Commands*, 6.
7. Karen Burton Mains, *Open Heart, Open Home,* 25.

Chapter Eight

1. John MacArthur, *MacArthur Study Bible*, II Corinthians 5:9-10.
2. Ibid, verse 10.

Chapter Nine

1. Jay Adams, *Christian Living in the Home,* 32-33.
2. John MacArthur, *MacArthur Study Bible,* Matthew 18:21.
3. David Seamands, *Healing for Damaged Emotions,* 25.
4. Ibid, 26.
5. John MacArthur, *The Freedom and Power of Forgiveness,* 58.
6. J.B. Phillips, *The New Testament in Modern English,* Hebrews 12:15.
7. Robin Mark, "When it's all Said and Done".

Chapter Ten – None

Chapter Eleven

1. Gene Getz, *Building up one Another,* 92.
2. Ibid, 93.
3. W.E. Vine, *Expository Dictionary of New Testament Words,* 116.
4. Getz, *Building up one Another,* 94.
5. Mark Ross, "In Essentials, Unity; in Non-essentials, Liberty; in all Things, Charity".
6. Ibid.
7. Bill and Gloria Gaither, "Getting Used to the Family of God."

Chapter Twelve

1. Jay Adams, *Competent to Counsel,* 44.
2. Gene Getz, *Building up one Another,* 93.
3. Adams, *Competent to Counsel,* 45.
4. W.E. Vine, *Expository Dictionary of New Testament Words,* 116.

Chapter Thirteen

1. Gene Getz, *Building up of one Another,* 99.
2. Ibid, 101.
3. John MacArthur, *The MacArthur New Commentary on Ephesians,* 247.
4. Ibid, 248.
5. Ibid, 249.
6. Ibid, 250.
7. Martin Lloyd Jones, www.mljtrust.org/free-sermons/book-of-ephesians/5.
8. James Lawrence, 3084 Christ is the Head of This House Framed Art.

Chapter Fourteen

1. William Barclay, *A-Z Quotes/William Barclay.*
2. William Barclay, *Daily Study Bible – The Gospel of John,* Volume 2, 194-195.
3. Gene Getz, *Building up one Another,* 111.
4. James Moffatt, *The Bible – James Moffatt Translation,* Job. 4:4
5. John White, *The Fight,* 216.
6. John MacArthur, *MacArthur Study Bible,* comment on Hebrews 3:13.
7. J.I. Packer, *God's Words,* 94.
8. giant-sequoia.com

Chapter Fifteen

1. Phillip Yancey, *Prayer – Does it Make any Difference?*, 303.
2. John MacArthur, *The MacArthur New Commentary – James,* 277.
3. Ibid, 278.
4. Phillip A. Keller, *A Shepherd Looks at Psalm 23,* 60.
5. Ibid, 62.

Chapter Sixteen

1. Charles R. Swindoll, *Improving Your Serve,* 18.
2. Ibid, 20.
3. John MacArthur, *MacArthur Study Bible,* John 13:4-5.
4. David Jeremiah, *Improving Your Serve,* 43. (Taken from Ruth Harms Calkin, *Tell me Again, Lord, I Forget.*).
5. Gene Getz, *Building up one Another,* 70.

Chapter Seventeen

1. Reissig, Courtney, "To Love is to be Vulnerable."
2. Warren Wiersbe, *The Bible Exposition Commentary,* Volume 2, 178-179.
3. Ibid, 180-181.
4. Warren Wiersbe, *The Bible Exposition Commentary,* Volume 1, 180.
5. D. James Kennedy, *This is the Life*, 13-14.

Works Cited

Adams, Jay. *Christian Living in the Home.* Phillipsburg, NJ: Presbyterian and Reformed Publishing Co., 1972.

Adams, Jay. *Competent to Counsel.* Grand Rapids, MI: Baker Book House, 1970.

Authorized King James Version Bible. Cambridge: Oxford University Press, 1967.

Barclay, William. "A-Z Quotes – William Barclay", page 1. inspiringquotes.u.s. 2020.

Barclay, William. *The Daily Study Bible: Gospel of John,* Volume 2. Philadelphia: Westminster Press, 1958.

Barclay, William. *The Daily Study Bible: Letters to the Galatians and Ephesians.* Philadelphia: Westminster Press, 1958.

Blackaby, Henry. *Experiencing God – Knowing and Doing the Will of God.* Nashville: B & H Publishing Group, 2007.

Bonhoeffer, Dietrich. *Life Together*: *The Classic Exploration of Christian Community.* New York: HarperCollins Publishers, 1954.

Bridges, Jerry. *True Fellowship.* Colorado Springs: Navpress, 1985.

Butterfield, Rosario. *The Gospel Comes with a House Key.* Wheaton, IL: Crossway Books, 2019.

Calkin, Ruth Harms. *Tell me Again, Lord, I Forget.* Elgin, IL: David C. Cook Publishing Co., 1974.

Callen, James. *Love one Another in Christ: Christian Example from the Early Church.* Blog: toliveischrist.com, 2019.

English Standard Version Bible. Wheaton, IL: Crossway Books, 2001.

Gaither, Gloria and William J. "Getting Used to the Family of God." *Hymns for the Family of God.* Nashville, TN: Paragon Associates, Inc., 1976.

Getz, Gene. *Building up one Another.* Wheaton, IL: Victor Books (division of SP Publications), 1981.

Getz, Gene. *Loving One Another.* Wheaton, IL: Victor Books (division of SP Publications), 1979.

Getz, Gene. *Sharpening the Focus of the Church.* Chicago: Moody Press, 1974.

Keller, Phillip A. *A Shepherd Looks at Psalm 23.* Grand Rapids, MI: Zondervan Publishing House, 1970.

Kennedy, D. James. *This is the Life.* Glendale, CA: Gospel Light Publications, 1973.

Lawrence, James. 3084 "Christ is the Head of This House" Framed Art. Amazon.com.

Lloyd Jones, Martin. www.mljtrust.org/free-sermons/book-of-ephesians/5.

MacArthur, John. *The Freedom and Power of Forgiveness.* Wheaton, IL: Crossway Books (a division of Good News Publishers), 1998.

MacArthur, John. *The MacArthur New Commentary: Ephesians.* Chicago: Moody Press, 1986.

MacArthur, John. *The MacArthur New Commentary: James.* Chicago: Moody Press. 1998.

MacArthur, John. *The MacArthur Study Bible.* Nashville: Thomas Nelson Publishers, 2006.

Maims, Karen Burton. *Open Heart, Open Home.* Elgin, IL: David C. Cook Publishing Co., 1976.

Mark, Robin. "When it's all Said and Done*" Days of Elijah: The Worship Songs of Robin Mark.* Provident Music Distribution, 2006.

Moffatt, James. *The Bible – James Moffatt Translation.* New York and London: Harper and Brothers, 1935.

New International Version Bible. Grand Rapids, MI: Zondervan Corporation. 1978.

New King James Version Bible. Edinburgh: Thomas Nelson, Inc. 1982.

Packer, J.I. *God's Words.* Downers Grove, IL: InterVarsity Press. 1981.

Phillips, J.B. *The New Testament in Modern English.* London: Geoffrey Bles, 1963.

Piper, John. Ask Pastor John Column. "The Holy Kiss – Relevant Today or Not?" *Desiring God 3* December 2015. http.www.desiringgod.org.

Reissig, Courtney. "To Love is to be Vulnerable." *Christian Living*, 8 Aug. 2013, p.1.

Ross, Mark. "In Essentials, Unity; in Non-essentials, Liberty; in all Things, Charity.*" Tabletalk Magazine,* 1st September 2009.

Schaeffer, Francis A. *The Mark of the Christian.* Downers Grove, IL: InterVarsity Press, 1970.

Schultz, Charles M. *Happiness is a Warm Blanket, Charlie Brown.* New York: Simon and Shuster, 2011.

Seamands, David. *Healing for Damaged Emotions.* Colorado Springs, CO: David C. Cook Publishing Co., 1981.

Smith, J. Warren. "See How These Christians Love one Another". *Christian History Magazine #105: Christianity in Early Africa,* 2013.

Strauch, Alexander. *The Hospitality Commands.* Littleton, CO: Lewis and Roth Publishers, 1993.

Swindoll, Charles R. *Improving Your Serve.* Waco, TX: Word, Inc., 1981.

Tenney, Merrill. *John, the Gospel of Belief.* Grand Rapids, MI: Eerdmans Publishing Co., 1953.

The Living Bible. Wheaton: Tyndale House Publishers, 1971.

The New English Bible. Cambridge: Oxford University Press, 1970.

Vine, W.E. *An Expository Dictionary of New Testament Words.* Old Tappan, NJ: Fleming H. Revell Co., 1966.

Wiersbe, Warren. *The Bible Exposition Commentary.* Volumes 1 and 2. Wheaton, IL: Victor Books (a division of Scripture Press), 1994.

White, John. *The Fight.* Downers Grove, IL: InterVarsity Press, 1978.

Yancey, Phillip. *Prayer – Does it Make any Difference?"* Grand Rapids, MI: Zondervan, 1981.